Audacious Faith

Audacious Faith

Malcolm W. Baxter

New Wine Press

New Wine Ministries
PO Box 17
Chichester
West Sussex
United Kingdom
PO19 2AW

Unless otherwise stated, Scripture quotations are taken from The Holy Bible, New International Version. Copyright © 1973, 1978, 1984 by International Bible Society. Used by permission of Hodder and Stoughton Limited.

NLT – The Holy Bible, New Living Translation, copyright © 1996. Used by permission of Tyndale House Publishers, Inc., Wheaton, Illinois, 60189. All rights reserved.

ISBN 978-1-905991-05-1

Typeset by CRB Associates, Reepham, Norfolk
Cover design by CCD, www.ccdgroup.co.uk
Printed in Malta

DEDICATION

*This book is dedicated to my wife Lynette,
whom I love with all my heart.
Thank you for running alongside me,
on our own journey of Audacious Faith.*

CONTENTS

Acknowledgments   9

Introduction   11

Chapter 1   **Looking for Love** (John 4:4–42)   15

Chapter 2   **Dumb and Dumber** (Mark 7:31–36)   23

Chapter 3   **Be My Guest** (Luke 19:1–9)   35

Chapter 4   **Mad as Hell** (Mark 5:1–20)   45

Chapter 5   **Blind Faith** (Mark 10:46–52)   57

Chapter 6   **The Big Issue** (Mark 5:21–34)   69

Chapter 7   **Untouchable** (Luke 5:12–14)   79

Chapter 8   **Presumed Dead** (Luke 7:11–16)   91

Chapter 9   **Making a Stink** (Luke 7:36–50)   101

Chapter 10 **Nailed** (Luke 23:26–43)   115

About the Author   125

ACKNOWLEDGMENTS

It was on my birthday in May 2006 that Lynette, my wife, sat me down, eye-balled me and told me, "Start writing or else".

This was the culmination of a campaign of nudges that evolved into fairly severe kicks up the behind, by her and the rest of our family: Bethany, Aaron, Joseph and Gabrielle. She had booked me a room in a B & B as a birthday gift and sent me on my way. I returned home two days later with the first chapter.

I *could not* have written this book without God's help and probably *would not* have written it without my family's relentless "encouragement". Thanks, guys, for your support and for releasing me to write on our all too precious days off. You know that I love you *all* beyond words.

A huge thank you also goes to Alison Cyprianos for her excellence in proof reading and Eugene Delport for his patient challenges to my punctuation and for his encouragement. Thank you also to Trevor and Avril Abrahams for the generous loan of your home at Bettys Bay. My time there contributed significantly to the priming of the pumps of creativity. Thanks also to Craig Kube and Aaron Baxter for their time and contributions.

Finally, to Tim Pettingale whose early encouragement and advice spurred me on to the finish line – thank you.

INTRODUCTION

There is something I love about airports. That the lives of people from all over the globe intersect, just for a moment, fills me with fascination. Those diverse threads of humanity weave around each other, but without connection. This snapshot moment doesn't give anyone the opportunity to tell the stories that make up the fabric of their life, indeed, that makes them who they are. The emptied departure lounge bears hollow testimony to the fact that we have all successfully managed to move on without knowing how any of us got there.

When we do take a moment to share, we realise that we are not as distant from each other as perhaps we first thought. Somehow there are echoes of my story in yours and vice-versa. It was with this thought in mind that I began to think about certain characters in the Bible. We often brush by them with little thought as to the possible backgrounds of their encounters with Jesus.

The characters' pasts are obviously fictionalised in this book, whilst sticking closely to the biblical rendition. Momentarily, they allow us to meander up and down the streets of what might have been their life and expose us to their humanity – helping us to realise that just as our stories can bridge the gap of geography or culture, the echo of theirs can call out across the centuries to touch ours. Almost forgetting they are from another era, we no

longer dismiss them as distant or irrelevant because somehow
we relate to their pain.

Each chapter stands alone, but there is definitely a common
thread. Firstly (with perhaps one exception) *audacious faith* was
displayed by somebody. Secondly, their meeting with Jesus
changed everything.

As a writer it is my desire that you be entertained. I hope
many of you will gain a fresh perspective on some very familiar
stories. However, if that is all that happens I will be disappointed.
My heart is that these candy-coated biblical accounts, with their
application, will reach into your life and give you permission to
be honest about yourself and *your* story. I believe that honesty
will be the key which opens the door to the possibility of hope
and the beginning of healing. I also believe that this book will be
a tool that will help us to say things to others that are sometimes
difficult to say. I trust it will help us to connect and pave the way
to further conversations.

Each account you read is about a journey to a miracle, but
most importantly it's about a journey to Someone. That
Someone is Jesus and my hope is that He who initially appears
on the horizon as some distant historical figure will meet with
you on the pages of this book.

These stories are fact woven into fiction. Every key character
you meet is a *real* person, imperfect and ordinary, with real issues
– even if I've given them a fictional name where the Bible is
silent. Their encounter with Jesus and the subsequent results are
factual, eye-witness accounts of transformed lives.

This may seem a little weird at first, but you know what? Most
of our lives are facts that have become entangled in fiction.
Maybe there is a huge gap between the person you were born to
be and the person you have become. Maybe we are yet to see the
real you. Jesus helps us to pick through our lives and separate
the fact from the fiction. In Him only is it possible to become

who you are destined to be. I am not saying that journey will be easy, but then again (as you will read) it is one that is very possible to navigate successfully ... especially when you have audacious faith.

CHAPTER 1

LOOKING FOR LOVE
(John 4:4–42)

She rolled out of bed and quickly drew the coarse top blanket around her. Tousled hair limply framed her face. Her once eye-catching beauty had faded, and even in the dim morning light you could see that the years had etched their story on her face.

Scooping the cloth that hung over the tiny window to one side, the first of the sunlight darted across the room and fell unceremoniously on the snoring form that lay in the bed. The fresh light illuminated the beads of sweat that had formed on his head and torso and he grunted and rocked until, like a scurrying insect, he turned to escape the glare.

She looked at him, like she had many times before, but today it was as though she was seeing him for the first time. As she stared she became aware of the haunting barrenness in her soul. Its icy darkness sent a familiar chill down her spine. She had been here before – the set and the characters changed, but the script was the same and she always played the leading role. Boy meets girl, girl swept into a white water fury of passion and promises. Boy gets what he wants – girl doesn't! Five husbands later and now this guy! She had longed for love, pledged by her parents at fifteen to, as she thought, a kindly man many years her senior. He divorced her for not bearing him a son. Somewhere between husbands two and three she decided she wouldn't be used again and so started using men and discarding them as she had been discarded.

Letting go of the makeshift curtain the room was once again plunged into the dank dimness, but the feeling would not go away. She should go to get water. It was going to be hot today. She became aware of the muffled sounds of a town waking. Women's voices faded in, reached a crescendo as they passed the door, only to fall away as they made their way to the well. Usually she'd be fine, throwing back her shoulders and strutting to the well, shrugging off the comments and stares. What was different about today she didn't know, but for some reason she just couldn't stomach it. *"I'll go later,"* she thought.

The decision brought relief but at the same time a quiet desperation pierced her soul. Was she losing it? Maybe. Were there cracks forming in the emotional dam that had been years in the making? The thought was unbearable. She had lost herself in all the things that she had become. How could she turn back now? Yet there really had to be more to life than this. Not that she had any particular reason to hope, but there it was, an un-suppressible something that enabled her to cling to a dream that things could be different. Perhaps it was God who fanned the embers of her dream? He seemed so distant though and she pondered how wonderful it must be to talk to Him face to face.

Snapped back to reality by a hoarsely spoken invitation to come back to bed was all she needed to uproot from the spot and slip outside to make a fire for breakfast.

She busied herself all morning until, tired and parched, she remembered she hadn't yet fetched water. It was as though the city nodded like a tired child wearied by its play. The heat, as always, had taken its toll and the hum of frantic flies filled the air. At least she was unlikely to have to wait her turn or run the gauntlet of those glances. The thought of the walk there and back gave her no joy and she sighed as she stooped to lift the clay jar onto her hip.

As she stepped outside a dog half lifted its head, but allowed it to flop again on its paw, as if the brief glance had drained its last drop of strength. In the distance children played in the dirt, but the streets were gradually emptying for lunch and siesta.

It was hot! The sun scorched the earth and rebounded in waves that blurred the vision and made the eyes squint. As she approached the well, her heart sank. There was someone there. She wanted to turn back but couldn't. She needed the water. Things got worse as she realised the distant figure was a man . . . a Jew. *Maybe I should turn back*, she thought, but you know what? He won't even give me the time of day, so I'll draw my water and be on my way.

As she came close to the well, she knew He was looking at her. She didn't look at Him, but she knew. She found herself irritated. *What's He looking at?* she thought and carried on about her business like she hadn't noticed. She stole a glance when she thought He might not notice. He wasn't attractive, He certainly wasn't her type. But she found herself fascinated that He didn't look at her in the same way that other men did. He wasn't leering or mocking – He looked like He cared. She wasn't used to it and didn't like it. Besides, why should He really be different from anyone else. They all seem like that in the beginning. She was flustered, told herself to get a grip and then it happened – He spoke to her. She was completely knocked sideways. So much so, that she wondered if she'd imagined it, but no, He *had* spoken to her and asked for a drink of water.

All that life had taught her was sent into a tail spin. This shouldn't be happening. Her heart was racing and, not knowing what else to do, she resorted to the lead role she knew so well.

'Sir, You are a Jew and I am a Samaritan woman . . . and *You* are asking *me* for a drink?'

Hearing the words come out of her mouth, she sounded unnecessarily brazen and harsh and immediately regretted it. She braced herself for a rebuke.

The man seemed unmoved. Brushing it aside He said, "If you understood the gift God has for you and who I am, you wouldn't be making those comments; you'd come rushing to get what you've been longing for all your life ... living water and I can give it to you."

(*Who is this man? He speaks to me like I'm human and not a dog.*) She was thrilled and soothed by the sound of His voice. It calmed her fears, stirred her soul and, warmed by His gentleness, her heart began to thaw. The script no longer seemed to fit, but it was the only one she knew. Knowing He wouldn't want to use anything she had brought, she commented,

"You want water yet you have nothing to draw with. Besides, where are You going to get this 'living water'? Do You somehow think that You are greater than Jacob, who gave us the well in the first place?"

She was missing the point and knew it. First, He wanted water from her. Now, He had water for her. She was confused and intrigued. Was He trying to get her to see beyond what she could see, taste and touch?

"Receiving this 'living water' means you will never be thirsty again," He said.

"Great! I'm sick of fetching water every day. Give me *that* water so that I won't be thirsty anymore."

The smirk that remained on her face when the words were done, shrivelled and died in an instant. In this brief pause everything changed. She looked into His eyes and saw herself in nauseating Technicolor.

"Fetch me your husband," He said.

Unsuccessful in her attempt to look casual, she said, "Err ... I don't have a husband."

"That's right! In fact, you've had *five* husbands, excluding the lover you're with now."

In that moment the world stopped and she would have got off, but shock had glued her sandals to the spot. She couldn't remember the last time she blushed, but she was blushing now, deep and hot!

There was no point in objecting; it was all true! Unmasked and ashamed, her head dropped. In Samaria everybody knew something about her, but this was the first time that somebody had known everything. She'd been exposed and vulnerability glazed her eyes.

Mouth dry, the words did not come easily but she said, "Look ... I know You're a man of God and I'm a mess and I don't usually talk about this, but You know what? I do believe in God and that there is someone coming, His Son, in fact, who will deliver me from this."

Feeling compelled to lift her head she did so; He caught her eye and she didn't look away.

"You're looking at Him!" He said.

Gentle yet powerful, His words washed her and invaded her soul. He smiled. That smile smashed through her darkness and, with oxyacetylene precision, cut away the things that for so long had held her captive. All her life she'd looked for love and now, for the first time, she found herself in its warm, liberating embrace.

She hardly dared to believe it was possible, but this man was unexplainably, unmistakably different. He knew everything about her and accepted her anyway. Her days of hiding and trading her body for a cheap, tacky imitation of love were over. She was clean, she was free and He knew it!

Laughter flowed from His smile as He watched her, according to plan, leave everything and run back to town. Rushing from door to door she wanted everyone to meet a man who knew everything about her. The silent streets began to teem with life as people poured from their homes in response to the commotion. Some rubbed their eyes and looked irritated to be disturbed from their siesta. This was particularly true when they saw *who* had disturbed them. Annoyance turned to abuse.

"She's drunk!" someone shouted.

"Crazy more like!" came the retort, which brought ripples of laughter, but some tilted their heads in curiosity.

"Wait!" someone insisted, "Something's happened to her – she's different."

A tidal wave of awareness broke over them that silenced their scorn and filled them with wonder. Could this radiant woman really be the one they thought they knew?

Silence fell and seizing the moment she said, still slightly panting, "Come and meet Him. He's still there."

Under the influence of wonder, they moved towards the well. Had they been given the option, they may not have chosen this particular messenger, but they could not deny the change that had taken place in her life. It was obvious!

They came to meet Him because, whatever it was she had, they wanted. They also needed someone to know everything about them and love them anyway. He did!

I don't know whether you've ever found yourself looking for love in all the wrong places. I know I have. When that void is there, we try to fill it with all kinds of stuff. This woman tried to find it in the arms of men, only to be disappointed over and over. You see, sex can never fill the gap. Neither can drugs, nor alcohol, nor food, nor soap operas – they only anaesthetise the pain for a little while, but never leave us respecting ourselves in the morning. As the unnamed woman navigated the waters of her disappointment, she refused to stop believing that things could change.

I don't know for sure, but (indulge me for a minute) I think Jesus turned up on the pages of her life at just the right time. I think He leaned on the well that day because He was waiting for her. God heard her heart scream out from the middle of her mess and had to meet with her. She didn't have to pretend anymore.

Have you ever paused to wonder how amazing it would be to stop pretending? Probably not ... and even if you did, it wouldn't be for long. That line of thinking usually leads to depression, because we can't find our way out of the maze.

Some of us have pretended for so long that we don't even realise that we are pretending anymore. We've tried to make a dash for freedom and found ourselves awash in a sea of regret, because we actually did reach out in trust, only to be mauled in the process. Many at that point accept the glass case that cynicism offers. From there we can observe the world and almost feel like we are part of what is going on, but no one can get in to hurt us again. And nursing our pain, we never come out to play.

Some live their lives changing the set and the characters, but remain trapped in a repetitive plot. We run around in circles creating mess and clearing it up again. Some families do this for generations, three steps forward and four steps back.

Our leading lady was trapped in a similar cycle. Using the same old methods to deal with the same old problems and getting the same old results.

There's a saying, "If you lie down with dogs you get up with fleas." Jesus knows how you got the fleas and He doesn't ask you to get rid of them before He loves you. However, in loving you, He won't deny they exist either. He won't duck the "five husbands and a lover" issues of your life! He doesn't condemn you, but simply points out that there is the possibility of a flea-free existence. And becoming aware of your bitten, irritated, infected life, you may find that an attractive option.

In discovering Jesus you'll also find there is a plan for your life. It has always been there and when you realise it, you'll show the dog the door and lie down in green pastures.

Locked within a broken woman trapped in a vicious circle, was someone able to influence a town. An appointment with the man at the well liberated her and the treasure within.

Our heroine runs uninvited down the streets of your life to ask you to come and meet a man called Jesus. "He has an appointment with you!"

The buried treasure within awaits liberation. Can it be possible that someone, knowing everything about you ... could love you?

He does!

CHAPTER 2

DUMB AND DUMBER
(Mark 7:31–36)

Adrenaline surging through my system, there was no time for words, I just managed to grab a handful of the young man's shirt and yank him backwards. Eyes wide, his bewildered face stared at me for a moment until he saw the horse and chariot that would have mowed him down whiz by and I watched realisation dawn as he pondered on what might have been.

I released my grip on his clothing and tried to knock out the crumpled bulge that resembled some hideous growth on his back. The lump imploded, but the impression remained.

"You were nearly killed," I said.

With no visible response, he turned his eyes away and his body followed.

"Oh thanks, you saved my life," I said sarcastically but there was nothing. He just kept walking.

Why I found myself so indignant at this guy's attitude, I don't know, but a simple "thank you" would have cost him nothing. Running up to him, I once again grabbed a fist full of clothing and span him around. The young man jumped and was clearly in disbelief that this could happen twice in such quick succession. This time, however, there was no angry horse . . . just an angry me.

"You could at least have said 'thank you'," I barked, grabbing hold of his shoulders to drive home my displeasure.

A quizzical look soon emerged from his stunned expression. He scrunched and then flickered his eyes as one does when one is using much effort and twisted his mouth as he tried to talk, but all that came out was grunts, garble and a spray of saliva.

"Deaf as a post," I heard a voice say.

It was my turn to be startled. I looked to see from where this chirped information had come and noticed the old woman now standing very close. Uninvited, she continued to speak, "You won't get a bit of sense out of him."

"Is he yours?" I asked.

"Heavens no," she laughed.

"So how do you . . . ?"

"He lives near me," she interrupted.

Relaxing my grip on his shoulders, I was feeling embarrassed as I realised that I must be dealing with some kind of half-wit (and he was probably thinking the same of me).

As soon as I let him go, he (perhaps not surprisingly) bolted!

"Oh, he'll be fine," said the woman with a cursory wave of her blue-veined hand and off she went.

The whole event was quite bizarre. No wonder I didn't come into town often. I much preferred to roam the quiet hillsides with my sheep. Town was a place where, to my mind, one came only when absolutely necessary and left as soon after arrival as possible. Today's events only confirmed my opinion. People complicated my life. The less time I was around them the better. Alone with the sheep and the elements, I could talk to God and live at peace. But, from time to time, the need to release money forced me from the hills and I'd buy and sell a few of the live-stock to purchase essential provisions. I would spend the night at an inn and at first light I'd be on my way.

Tired and hungry I began to make my way to my usual hostelry. It was a little out of the way, but I was eagerly anticipating its quiet warmth as I meandered along. Humming softly to myself, I walked through the dark alley adjoining the street where I was due to stay.

The blow to the back of my head caused darkness to rush in and briefly overwhelmed me, leaving me sprawling headlong in the dirt. Waves of nausea ebbed and flowed, as I was kicked again and again in the ribs. Writhing in pain, I sought to avoid further blows, but they were relentless. In the dust and gloom, I couldn't see anybody. Some object made connection with my face and I was plunged once again into unconsciousness.

Eventually emerging, I became aware of the bitter copper and salt taste of blood which was the overture to an unfolding nightmare of excruciating pain. From head to foot my body throbbed!

My money! I thought (and half muttered).

Spontaneously I moved my hand to search for it, but was arrested sharply by a jolt of pain. I continued more cautiously reaching and patting for the linen bag that had contained the fruit of the day's business, but of course it had gone! Anger burned through my frame, releasing the energy to try to get up, but again I was thwarted by bruised and what must have been broken ribs, causing me to cry out in pain and frustration.

Dirt hung thick and hazy in the air and in its fog and my confusion I became aware of somebody near me. Fearing the worst I lashed out as best I could.

"I've got nothing left! I've got nothing left!" I croaked.

The one near me said nothing but grabbed my flailing arms and held them firmly, but gently, until I stopped struggling. Relief, shock and pain combined to release hot, stinging tears as I realised whoever it was, they were there to help.

"They've got my money. They've taken everything." I said.

Three rough finger tips were tenderly placed on my lips, indicating that I should be silent. Hooking his hand and pulling his sleeve over it, he gently dabbed the blood from around my nose and mouth.

We battled, but eventually, my arm around his shoulders, he managed to get me to my feet. As my world spun, I leaned heavily upon him. Drunk with pain I didn't even think to challenge where he was taking me, I just allowed him to take my weight as we shuffled and hopped our way along.

Kicking open a door after what seemed a very long way, the room we entered was in pitch darkness. He led me to a bed and eased me down upon it, before gently swinging around my legs. After an initial gasp from pain, I felt a degree of relief in being horizontal and as I lay there, a galaxy of shooting stars rained before my eyes and ushered in the darkness once again.

My mother, dabbing cool water with an itchy cloth on my face, was laughing. I began to smile back, but that hurt, then frame by frame I was brought back to the reality that my mother had been dead for years, but there *was* a cloth dabbing my face in a dimly lit room. Who was it? Where was I?

I took hold of the wrist belonging to the hand which was holding the cloth and held it steady, whilst my eyes began to focus and I tried to remember. I was battling to make sense of the merry-go-round of thoughts in my head. A face I did not recognise at first became clear. A pulsing hammer in the back of my head reminded me what had happened.

"Who are *you*?" my voiced rasped, as the words clawed their way through the dirt that clung to the back of my throat. There was no sound . . . just that hand with the cloth moving as though to continue with its task. I held it steady.

"Who *are* you?" I repeated, now with a little more strength.

Still nothing! Then with some force, the wrist freed itself from my grip and a cry of intelligible frustration left the lips that hovered above my head. In an instant I was aware that this was the ungrateful half-wit I'd tried to help. A barrage of fear-fuelled thoughts flashed up on the screen of my mind. I was alone with him and God only knows where.

My body could in no way match my mind's agility. Though everything within me wanted to move, it successfully rebelled against the desire. Logic filtering through the panic brought me to my senses – revenge would have left me in the alley, not brought me to lie on this bed. My new theory brought some comfort, but left me feeling vulnerable nonetheless.

After he'd finished with the cloth, he disappeared for a while and returned to pull me out of my semi-conscious state by pressing a cup of warm broth to my sore lips. At first it felt good to replace the taste of stale blood, but the coughing, spluttering and ensuing pain soon made the pleasure not worth the price.

A difficult and disturbed night yielded to dawn. My face was so swollen it was difficult to open my eyes. Battling with focus and the light, it took time to see who was sitting on the edge of the bed. Expecting to see the half-wit, you can imagine my surprise when I saw a young lady. Imagining I was hallucinating, I closed my eyes and on opening them again she was still there. Raven-black ringlets danced with her every move around the soft pink of her cheeks. Piercing, blue, smiling eyes glinted in the rays of the morning sun. Taking a shallow but sharp intake of breath I tried to talk, but she pipped me to the post, "Don't try to talk."

My lips were swollen and cracked, making articulate speech difficult.

"But . . . who are you?" I slurred.

"My brother brought you home last night. What happened?"

"Your brother?"

Somewhat embarrassed, I mumbled my story, as she listened intently. As I drew to a conclusion, I noticed the half-wit come in the room. He smiled at me a little nervously and I reciprocated, but he would not have noticed as my swollen lips hardly moved.

"Mark (it was the first time I'd heard his name or thought about him having one), fetch me water," she said whilst gesticulating with her hands. Without hesitation he left.

"I thought he was deaf," I said,

"Yes, but not stupid," she replied in such a way that brought the conversation to an abrupt conclusion.

Mark returned with the water and seemed thrilled to be of use. His sister used it to bathe me, and though *she* may have been nicer to look at, her brother was certainly gentler!

"Maybe I could at least know the name of my torturer?" I said.

"Anna," she replied and rubbed a little harder for effect, which in turn made me gasp with pain (and a cautious chuckle). Some smaller children (no doubt drawn by the screams) came to secretly peek, but someone gave their position away with a snigger. My nurse's head spun around and hissed with mock sternness, causing them to squeal and scurry away like insects escaping a sudden burst of light. When she turned back, a smile tugged at her lips.

As I convalesced, I found myself wrapped up in the world of my new and silent friend. One by one I met the family. Day by day as I grew stronger and the swelling decreased, they grew bolder. I spent less and less time alone. Tragedy had caused our paths to cross and time had tamed my prejudice. I would normally have considered myself much better off than Mark, so much was against him. Yet surrounded by the love, joy and acceptance of his family, it was I who felt poor.

"You have a visitor," Anna said loud enough to stir me from my siesta. Without further announcement, in walked one of the young men with whom I'd left the sheep. Drawn to town through concern regarding my long absence, he'd been asking around for days until eventually someone had given him directions to this house.

His concern, though, was somewhat overshadowed by great excitement regarding some character in town who was, apparently, doing miracles. The blind were seeing and cripples were walking and all this only a couple of streets away. They said His name was Jesus, He came from Nazareth and some thought Him to be the Messiah. The young man suggested that I go to Him as soon as possible and then maybe I could be healed and return with him to the flocks.

Mild interest quickly evolved into great excitement.

"Someone get Mark!" I screamed, "Quickly!"

The urgency in my voice brought Anna, dragging Mark behind her. I didn't even allow her to get any words out, I grabbed Mark and declared, "We're going to town". Ignoring all Anna's protests, I rushed (as best I could) out of the door to find this Jesus. The bewildered family all followed.

As we marched through the streets in search of the miracle-worker, we gathered quite a crowd, some family, some neighbours and some just plain curious came along for the ride.

As we negotiated the maze of streets, my body rebelled against the heat and premature burst of activity. The all too familiar nausea rose in my stomach and waves of pain hindered my progress. I stopped momentarily to lean on a wall and catch my breath. I could tell I was not looking good by the expressions of the people staring back at me.

Anna, confusion etched on her face, said, "What are you doing?"

Mark, drenched with sweat and concern, moved towards me and wiped my brow. Finding my voice I looked directly at Anna and said, "I'm not crazy . . . we need to get Mark to Jesus."

"We *need* to get back home!" (As though she had not heard) She echoed my tone firmly.

God knows, the way I was feeling, there was nothing I wanted more . . . well actually there was. If this Jesus was a healer, why couldn't He heal Mark?

"We have to find Him," I said and, ignoring the protests, I pushed on, but this time with Mark, supporting me by my elbow.

And then as we turned the next corner, there He was walking towards us, Him with His crowd and me with mine. How I knew it was Him I'm not sure, except that there was something just wonderful about being near Him. It was like a special moment that you never wanted to end. Breathless from exertion *and* excitement, I cried out as I pushed Mark into Jesus' path.

"Please put Your hands on him and make him well like You did the others," I begged. Within moments the crowd joined me in my pleading.

Jesus stopped and looked at Mark intently. Mark transfixed . . . meekly following as Jesus drew him to one side.

He put His fingers in Mark's ears, spat and then touched his tongue. Mark gave a brief sideways glance at me, which seemed to say "Why have you brought me to this lunatic?"

His gaze, though, returned to Jesus as He let out a loud sigh and cried out "Be opened!"

Immediately, my silent friend lifted his hands to cover his ears, as someone who'd just heard a loud bang. Eyes wide he slowly lifted them off and spontaneously began to speak clearly as we all stood, rooted to the spot and stunned. Mark was crying out coherently over and over,

"Praise God! Praise God!" Suddenly aware that he was hearing and speaking, his voice cracked and he began to sob as he touched his lips and ears in amazement.

Anna, flushed, with tears streaming down her face, pushed through to get to him as the crowd pressed in and marvelled, asking loudly amongst themselves and speaking of Jesus, "Who could this man be?"

Jesus was being moved along and away from us by the flow of the crowd. Still moving He glanced back over His shoulder and our eyes met. The distance in no way hindered the intensity of their impact. I found myself overwhelmed with a sense that everything was going to be alright and just before He disappeared around the corner He winked at me, as if to acknowledge that He'd seen the "penny drop".

I turned around to look straight into Anna's tear-stained face. "Thank you," she said as though she'd been holding it in for a long time and wanted to get it off her chest.

"For what?" I replied, "This was God!" Staring into her eyes and seeing something more than just my reflection I said, "I should be leaving."

"Should you?" she responded.

After a long and bashful pause I said, "Not really!"

She smiled and I couldn't stop myself from smiling back.

We rejoined our hero as his now incessant voice continued to praise God and amaze the crowd.

Noticing me near him he threw himself at me and hugged me tightly. Eventually standing back he said, "This is amazing!"

Hearing him speak made me smile and I looked into Anna's eyes. "Yes it is . . . isn't it?" Now it was her turn to be bashful.

Melting into the crowd we began our journey home and Mark talked all the way!

Having a voice means more than just having the ability to speak. Words have weight, value and purpose. Our words are generally taken notice of, but just as there are many who *can* hear but do not listen, there are many who *can* speak, yet have no voice. All around us are the unuttered screams of those who long for their desperation to be picked up on someone's "radar".

The unsettled child, irritatingly clingy and failing to thrive, because she dreads the improper advances of someone who presses a finger to her lips and terrorises her into silence.

Mr Next Door, respectable and married to that lovely woman who is devoted, diligent and desperately lonely. Her long sleeves conceal the black and blue souvenirs of yesterday's beating,

delivered with the promise it will never happen again. But it does
… it always does.

The refugee, alone and a long way from home, runs through an
open door straight into the arms of hostility, desperation making
them easy pickings for maltreatment and exploitation.

The old widower (two blocks down, garden overgrown, pension
inadequate) shuffles silently to the shops and back. Many look
… yet no-one sees, as hopelessness treads on the fingers that
cling to life.

The abused, the bullied, the tormented and the just plain
ignored sit opposite us, queue with us, live next door and
generally do life with us, their fear and silence cloaking their pain.

A few years ago, we ran a campaign from our church which
reached out to our community. A group of us went, gardening
tools in hand, to offer our meagre but enthusiastic skills free of
charge. This offer was usually met with surprise and no small
amount of suspicion, as we were working in a place where few did
anything for nothing. On one of these visits we knocked on the
door of a woman who was stunned at our offer to do the garden
but she accepted. When we were done, she wept. It was a slightly
worrying reaction (however, we were fairly confident that we
hadn't dug up her prize pansies). She told us that she had lain in
bed the night before sobbing, because a third long-term relation-
ship had come to an end. In the midst of her pain she had cried
out to God that she would believe in Him if someone, somewhere
would just show her some kindness. Our gardening team
knocked on her door the very next day. She wept with gratitude
and (even more) amazement, because she was having a hard
time believing that this was all just a coincidence.

Anguish will sometimes lift our cry to a frequency that only God
can hear and understand … and He does hear and He does
understand. Life has a way of serving us the kind of curve-ball
that leaves us crying out and making all kinds of promises to a

God of whom we would have possibly denied the existence of but moments earlier. God does answer our prayers, but not always in the way we would want. We turn away the gardening team, because we have told God *how* and *through-whom* we want Him to answer us.

He is not, however, a God who only listens when others don't. Our circumstances are often changed because He restores our voice. He gives us the strength and confidence beyond what we could produce ourselves to break the silence that has imprisoned us. Silence can give us a false sense of control – "if I keep sweeping it under the carpet, then just maybe . . . one day . . . it will all go away?" Speaking out is often not the easy option. It can be unpopular; it rocks the boat and may even intensify the pain. Blowing the whistle on an abusive boss may cost you your job, but it also might not. Leaving an intimidating and physically abusing husband will create all kinds of vulnerability and challenge, particularly if you are taking children with you. But you will also be opening up your world to choices . . . real choices. If you call out to God, He will help you. The moment you realise that God has created you for more than *this* and that you are worth more than what you've been going through; maybe then, you will begin to let God remove the gag that fear and intimidation has tied on you. No-one, least of all me, can make those kinds of choices for you. I do believe, however, that if you allow God to restore the lines of communication between you and Him first, then it will open up a myriad of possibilities.

God gives us a song of freedom to sing in the prison cell. God gives us the ability to confess the promise of light, whilst we sit in the darkness. Sometimes repeated disappointment will rob us of an ability to speak life into our circumstances. This is not about denial, nor is it about pretence. It's about using the power of the Word, God's Word, to create order in chaos. At creation . . . God spoke. The chaos became order. The Bible tells us that "The power of life and death is in the tongue." God has given us a voice and it is His intention that we use it to prophesy change into our circumstances.

Ezekiel, faced with the death and barrenness of the dry bones, was asked by God, "Can these bones live?" You see, we have to believe in the possibility of something, before we will speak to it in the right way. It is our confession that will either lead us nearer to ... or further away from the goal.

Ezekiel had the wisdom to set aside any doubts he was feeling and remember who it was that he was talking to. It has very little to do with what we feel and a whole lot to do with what God says. In Ezekiel's case, God said it through Ezekiel's mouth and called possibility out of impossibility.

For some who read this, the restoration of your voice will mean once again speaking out the things God has said, where doubt and disappointment have silenced you. Where you have shut up and put up with all kinds of rubbish, even now faith and confidence are rising again. Powerlessness is being weakened by the realisation that as you get up in the face of impossibility, you *can* speak to that mountain and see it cast into the sea in Jesus' name!

Others will be courageous enough to speak out for the first time and smash the wall of silence they have hidden behind. It's tough but when Moses came to God with all his excuses of why he couldn't, God reminded him who gave man his mouth and gives him the ability to speak. He then said, "Now go! I will be with you as you speak, and I will instruct you in what you say."

It is time to stop making excuses and believe that things really can be different. Moses' God is your God and maybe it is dumb to shut-up and put up, remaining locked up, when God can help you speak up ... and set you free.

CHAPTER 3

Be My Guest
(Luke 19:1–9)

His Father (God rest his soul) had always said to him, "You may be small and you may be ugly, but you'll always be rich!" And though his father was not a prophet, he wasn't far from the mark. It's just that he wasn't rich, he was *very* rich!

He had never intended working for Rome, but at least they gave him a job in spite of his size. He was tired of being picked on by *his* people.

"Stand up! Oh ... sorry ... you *are* standing."

"If ever we have an opening for puppets, we'll let you know ... " (followed by raucous laughter).

Children would quietly fall in behind him and mock him as he muttered to himself and shuffled along as fast as his little legs would carry him through the marketplace. Eventually the laughter of bystanders alerted him and he turned and chased, but they were always too fast and he was left to stand and curse, before once again shuffling and muttering on his way.

Well, who was laughing now? He'd been the object of fun his whole life, but now they would have to take him seriously. They'd have to respect him as they handed over their money, some for Rome and some for himself.

He hadn't got to where he was by chance. In fact, it was precisely because of his ruthless attitude and his flat refusal to give any kind of leniency on late payments (he always charged exorbitant interest to compensate for the inconvenience of reminding late payers) that had earned him promotion to Chief Tax Collector of the region.

He ate at the best restaurants, dressed in clothes made from the finest fabrics and was invited to the most prestigious parties, but for the most part he had stopped going to social events. He usually ended up just standing alone watching everyone else have fun and he didn't need to go to parties to be alone. He could do that all by himself at home.

This little man had made no small investment in his home, which was nothing short of palatial by local standards. He certainly had no qualms about taking all that he had made and rubbing it in the jealous, sneering faces of his neighbours. Here, in his self-made refuge, he would count his money and pore over his books and draw delight from his increasing wealth.

But, for all his material success, he was far from happy. Loneliness gnawed at his heart like a dog with a bone. He used his wealth and all its trappings to dull the pain of not having that for which he'd always longed – to feel valued, needed. Certainly there was a kind of artificial respect that he received from those who worked for him, but it was never from the heart and the truth was, if they could take him down, they would! He hated to be hated, but had long ago decided that in this life you have to fight fire with fire, an "eye for an eye and a tooth for a tooth".[1] The only way to survive is to always make sure you're a step ahead of the next man, to get him before he gets you and, if he has to go under in order for you to keep your head above water, so be it. It's about survival in a dog eat dog world.

Everyone he had ever trusted had let him down. As he began to make money, he began to make friends and while the wine and free food lasted, so did the friends. But he wasn't going to be used. So he dropped them all. He didn't need people like that around his life. Just as people had used him, he now used people. He went through servants like laundry. As he said, they were all worthless, lazy and no good, so he was better off without them. His life had become a cycle of hiring, firing and watching his own back (because if he didn't who would?) Nobody ever stayed around him for long, that is, with the possible exception of Rhoda.

On the edge of the seedier part of town there was a public house. This was a place where prostitutes, drunkards and fellow tax collectors met, where cheap wine and generous quantities of reasonable food were served. It was always filled with raucous laughter and shallow conversation, but he didn't go for any of those things.

Apart from the odd nod and grunt of greeting, he never mingled much anyway. Here he could sit in his usual place by the window and not feel judged. That's why he came and that's why he was here this evening. Everyone was pretending that everything was alright and with the passing of time and plenty of wine, the pretence was almost believable.

Rhoda, one of the barmaids, always wore the same dress, with the same two stains on the front. Her hair was mostly hidden under a scarf, apart from the few strands that escaped and hung shiny and black around her face. In her ears she wore an enormous pair of gold earrings (a gift from a drunken trader) that jangled and sparkled even in this dark, dank place. She had kind eyes and her smile would have been beautiful had she managed to keep all her teeth. However, nothing hindered her from revealing the two she had left, often, and without embarrassment.

"Good evening, Mr Zacchaeus, sir. How are you?" Rhoda inquired as he walked in.

Under any other circumstances and in any other place Zacchaeus would have found Rhoda unbearably upbeat, but somehow she knew exactly how to handle him. Not waiting for a response she said, "I've brought you your usual," as she placed the goblet on the table.

Zacchaeus found himself smiling in spite of himself. *I wonder how Rhoda always knew how to get the right kind of reaction from him*, he reflected momentarily.

There was no pretence, no airs and graces, what you saw was what you got with Rhoda. What he loved most about her was she treated him like a man. Whenever he was with her, he forgot he was small ... and he liked that!

She sat down opposite him, uninvited, and leaned forward over the table towards him. Looking around briefly before speaking, she said, "Have you heard about that carpenter's son from Nazareth?"

Zacchaeus, speaking for the first time, said, "No."

Glancing around again Rhoda moved in yet closer so that now Zacchaeus could not only feel her breath on his face, but also he could smell wine (and something else he wasn't sure about).

"They call Him Jesus and He was in *here*!" She sat back, but moved in again. "People say He's a Rabbi and some people even believe He's the Messiah, but I don't think that can be true, because He was in here mixing with our lot, I mean, I ask you."

"My dear Rhoda," Zacchaeus replied as he tried to move his head back and out of the direct firing line of her breath. "The man is from Nazareth and, therefore, clearly not all there!" Zacchaeus tapped his temple as he said it, just before taking a sip of wine.

"Well, I know Mr Zacchaeus sir, that's exactly what I thought. I mean, you know me, I don't usually go for those religious sorts. I mean you don't have to be round them for any time at all before you end up feeling like absolute ..."

"Thank you, Rhoda," Zacchaeus interjected.

"Yes, of course. Sorry, Mr Zacchaeus, but you know what I mean! He wasn't like that though. He didn't talk about God in a 'Do this, do that, be miserable for the rest of your life kind of way!' I mean, you know me, Mr Zacchaeus, sir. I'm not one to listen in on someone else's conversation . . . "

Zacchaeus would have responded at that point, but momentarily his concentration was broken by him concluding that the *other* smell on her breath was somewhere between garlic and sour milk. Satisfied with his conclusions his attention returned.

Rhoda, not noticing the brief lapse in concentration, continued, "But I just couldn't help listening to Him. He spoke of God as though He really cared about us and we weren't supposed to spend our whole lives just keeping Him off our backs. He said that God loved us right now, just as we were and that He wanted to be our friend. I mean '*our* friend', Mr Zacchaeus? I couldn't believe it! And then He said that *He* could show us the Way.

Some just laughed and slapped His back, but I couldn't help but like what He said. I caught the eye of one of the girls who was also listening to Him. When a drunk came and buried himself in her neck, she shoved him away, instead of giving a customer the come on. I knew exactly what she was feeling. Somehow, in being around Jesus, we felt like we were supposed to be more . . . that we were actually worth something."

"Rhoda?"

"Yes, Mr Zacchaeus, sir?"

"Precisely how much wine have you had? Because the way you're drivelling on, you are either drunk or as crazy as that carpenter's son. Now get me another drink."

"Oh, listen to me, Mr Zacchaeus, going on like I don't know what." She stood up and Zacchaeus, released from the blast of her breath, found he could breathe freely once again. He finished his wine and waved the glass.

"Let me get that wine for you." She started walking away and then stopped and briefly turned back, looking Zacchaeus square in the eye.

"It would be nice though, wouldn't it? You know? If it *were* true."

She didn't wait for his response, but whisked around and disappeared into the rowdy crowd.

The following day, whilst scurrying about his business, Zacchaeus noticed a crowd gathering and lining the street.

"What's happening?" he called out to someone.

"Jesus is coming!" they exclaimed.

"Jesus?" he thought to himself. Ever since Rhoda had spoken to him about Jesus, he hadn't been able to get Him out of his mind. He must catch a glimpse of Him. Zacchaeus ran up and down trying to squeeze in somewhere, but it was impossible. In frustration he looked up and noticed the sycamore fig tree. *"I know,"* he thought, *"I'll climb that!"* Well, what seemed like a good idea at the time soon became a huge challenge for those small arms and legs, but, with grit and determination, he managed to climb up, lodge himself in comfortably and prepare to enjoy his bird's-eye view. Not a moment too soon as it turned out. In the distance he could just make out someone who was the focus of everyone's attention. As Jesus was about to pass by, Zacchaeus was fascinated. *"I'd give half my wealth to spend some time with this man."* he thought. No sooner had the thought passed over his mind, than Jesus stopped under the tree and looked up, smiling from ear to ear.

Because Jesus was looking up, everyone else did too. Zacchaeus suddenly realised that here he was, the Chief Inspector of Taxes – up a tree. Now *this* was embarrassing!

People, beginning to realise who Jesus was looking at, just loved it and laughter ricocheted around the crowd.

"Thank goodness this guy doesn't know me," thought Zacchaeus.

(By now the laughter was so loud that Jesus had to raise His voice.)

"Zacchaeus, come down here quickly. I must be your guest today."

"*Oh no, oh no, He knows my name,*" thought Zacchaeus, withdrawing into the branches. He suddenly did a double take.

"Hey, He knows me. Jesus knows *my* name!"

To this day, he cannot remember getting down from the tree, but he does remember standing, looking up in to the face of Jesus. The laughter had stopped and there was an eerie silence of disgust and disbelief from the onlookers.

Why on earth would Jesus want to go to *his* home? hung unspoken in the atmosphere. It was now *their* turn to shuffle and mutter. But as for Zacchaeus, he felt ten feet tall.

"Shall we?" Jesus said, and they went to Zacchaeus' house.

No one ever knew what kind of exchange there was between the two of them, but whatever it was, Zacchaeus was never the same again. It was one hundred per cent proof joy that spilled over from Zacchaeus' life and splashed generosity on those around him.

"I'm going to give half my money to the poor," Zacchaeus said. Then (much to Jesus' amusement) he blinked, as the realisation of what he'd said hit him. People thought that he'd lost his mind as he was giving his money away, but he had never been saner.

"You know what, Jesus?" continued Zacchaeus, "If I have ripped off anybody I'm going to give them four times what I owe them."

"...*If* you've ripped off anybody?" Jesus interjected with a knowing look.

There was a brief but pregnant pause. Zacchaeus sniggered... and they both fell about laughing!

✢ ✢ ✢

We're not very good with different, are we? We live in a generation that has decided what the normal is and God help anybody who doesn't look like Barbie or Action Man. No longer just the pastime of the Hollywood elite, Joe Public is prepared to pay thousands to be nipped, tucked, lifted, increased, reduced and the plastic surgeons laugh all the way to the bank.

Now, don't get me wrong, if it's *that* important to you and you have the money, go ahead. I wouldn't stand in the way of something you perceive will make you happier and feel better about yourself. However, please do yourself a favour and go to someone who knows what they are doing. It may have been a bargain, but if you look like you are permanently caught in a wind tunnel, I, for one, have questions.

It's just that, in all this, isn't anyone just a little worried that we are so focused on externals? You may be sixty and look forty, but you are still you and a wrinkle free-life is not a problem-free life. In our preoccupation with physical perfection have we not lost the plot?

Intellectually most people agree that we are not defined by what we are physically, but we continue to live as though the opposite is true. People are chosen for their gifts, yes, as long as it's packaged in a marketable face and body. From pop stars to presidents we are too often hypnotised by what people look like rather than who they are.

There are many who cannot even begin to compete in this world – whether born that way, or maimed in life, they will never fit "the image". We rebuke our children for staring at "different", but maybe we should take a leaf out of their book, because if we looked long enough, we might eventually see a person.

And if it's not what we look like, it's what we've got! For the record, I do not buy into the pious poverty that some believe to be the mark of a "true" Christian. Zacchaeus was *very* wealthy and even after he met Jesus and given half his fortune away, this still left him wealthy (even if for the sake of argument, we have to drop the *very*) and that was fine with Jesus.

I believe that the reason Jesus wanted to introduce Zacchaeus to us was because He wanted to remind us that life is so much more than what you look like or what you have. You may have clawed yourself to success, "shown" all those who doubted you, but at what cost?

Jesus showed Zacchaeus that happiness was never going to be found by focusing inwardly, on me, mine, what I can get and stuff everyone else.

Zacchaeus did two things, which I believe made a massive difference to his life.

Firstly, he gave. "Well, he was rich!" I hear you cry. "He could afford to give." True, but not the point. There are many other examples in the Bible, be it a widow's mite, a few loaves and fish or a few drops of oil, where people did not give out of abundance, but gave anyway. Giving releases something . . . well . . . *us* for a start! It would appear that God is trying to teach us that the more we are a channel of His blessing, the more we will find what true riches are.

Secondly, Zacchaeus made restitution. Restitution is more than just "saying you're sorry". It's about paying back with interest anyone you have used or abused, or from whom you have inappropriately acquired things. Zacchaeus said he would pay four times what he owed. Of course there are some things for which we could never make restitution and, even if you do put your hand in your pocket, it may not make everything alright between you and them (though it might make a good start).

These things may not be comfortable to think about, but Jesus shows us that our internal world is important. In fact, if there is order there, then our external world seems to fall into place. However, if there is disorder there, it doesn't matter how good things are on the outside, it will never be enough. The significant changes in Zacchaeus' life cost him something. Some might say he paid too high a price, but it definitely seemed to Zacchaeus to have been worth it.

This chapter may have stirred a few things within you, even some sleeping dogs that you would be tempted to let lie. Maybe something's hidden in the closet that needs addressing. The cost may be too high or too challenging. "It's too late now," you say "too much water passed under the bridge." This may be true for some, but for others it is not too late and they *can* do something. It could be as simple as a letter, an email, a phone call, a cheque or something more, but it will be the beginning of a significant journey.

It is important to note that Jesus didn't send Zacchaeus off to do everything by himself. He was there with him, walking him through the process.

Jesus stands at the door and knocks, saying "I must be your guest *today*." He'll talk you and walk you through some things, which will help sort out your internal world. You will have to trust Him. It will cost you and you'll possibly have to make amends in some areas, but He promises no matter how difficult, He will be with you!

The question is ... will you let Him in?

Notes _____

1.   Exodus 21:24.

CHAPTER 4

MAD AS HELL
(Mark 5:1–20)

The sudden, agonizing scream that bounced around the hillside was not loud enough to make you jump, but it *was* haunting enough to make children pull closer to their mother and seek the kind of comfort that *only* a loving mother can bring. Whenever you heard it, you wanted it to stop and tonight was no exception.

"Make it stop, Mummy!" came the muffled cry.

She didn't really answer. Hannah stroked the back of the head of the child whose face was buried in her skirt.

"I know, baby, I know," she said, patting and stroking his head as she spoke.

Hannah stared at nothing in particular as she remembered a family, pitifully poor, living next door and a boy who was always a little bit different. His grandmother, a medium, was always making him wear fetishes and drink strange concoctions she had prepared. People just thought him strange, the odd one out, never quite fitting in. She remembered his sallow face and ever-shifting eyes. He always had a slightly frenzied look about him. But the thing that forever perplexed her was that the inside of his forearms were always scratched and never seemed to heal – a criss-cross of pink, red and the deep burgundy of dried blood.

She remembered one night, representative of many, when crowds had gathered to end his reign of terror. The flames of the torches dipped and danced as they tentatively, and with occasional bursts of boldness, moved in to catch their prey. The hunted backed away like a wounded lion, his eyes ablaze with fury and terror. Suddenly, they pounced. More than twenty men attempted to pin him down, but he, fighting with a strength that was not his own, tossed them aside, until by sheer weight of numbers they managed to hold him down. Clamping shackles and chains to his limbs, it seemed that this time they had got him. He fought at first of course, but then he began to cry, like a small child who had just had his toy snatched away.

Once they were sure he was restrained, the now brave crowd began to taunt him. Some mocked the noise of his cry, some spat at him and shook their fist angrily. The more tamed he seemed, the closer the crowd moved towards him. Children were encouraged with laughs when they threw stones at the captive, then ran back into the crowd.

The more they taunted, the more this beast of a man began to rage. The crowd laughed all the more as he attempted to pull apart the chains, his face red, eyes bulging, neck veins straining. There were guttural growls and grunts and then, with what sounded like the crack of a whip, the first chain went and the crowd, paralysed with shock, fell silent. It was not spoken but it hung in the air as potently as if it had been:

"Surely the other chain will hold!"

With another sudden crack! and then a clanking thud, chains hit the hardened earth. This time the man looked almost as shocked as everyone else. There was a split second of disbelief, before waves of hysteria scattered the crowd this way and that, whereupon he disappeared back to the tombs, released but far from free.

Another tormented scream lashed out that sent a shiver down the spine, and seeking to distract the bundle pressed into her hip, she, in a light and upbeat a manner said,

"Who wants hot milk?"

"Me, me, me" came the retort.

The night was clear and the moon was so bright it seemed to pulsate – a light breeze teased the branches of the olive trees.

Far in the distance, a figure darted and dived as though pursued, shouting,

"Get away, get away."

He paused only to punch his head several times and then put his hands over his ears before starting to run again. He ran and ran before falling and rolling many more times than the momentum of the fall would have caused. When at last he came to rest, he lay motionless, staring blankly into the night sky. His chest rose and fell and his matted hair adhered itself to the sweat that was now streaming down his face. Some ran into his eyes and, because it stung, it forced him to clamp them shut. The discomfort made him roll over and press his eyes into his forearm. Lying silent for only a moment he began to whimper pitifully, which quickly developed into a torrent of gut-wrenching tears. He cried so hard that he retched, but his empty stomach could produce nothing for all the effort. Finally, exhausted, he fell backwards and lay there, eyes once again staring, fixed and wide, white, sticky foam clinging to the corners of his mouth.

A raging thirst compelled him to stir. Quiet now, he made his way to the edge of the lake. He stooped to lap the water, but caught sight of his reflection in the unusually still shallows. He tilted his head from side to side, as a dog might, to make sense of what it is observing.

For a moment he forgot his thirst and saw the matted clumps of hair that hung now under their own weight around his face. The light was not good enough to see the bruising but he could see the swelling around the eyes and with uncommon tenderness he pulled his fingers over his skin. Suddenly he began to weep, now not uncontrollably but softly. Tears trickled as he seemed to respond to the dark sadness in the eyes that were being reflected back at him.

He sat on his haunches, wrapped his arms around his legs and gently rocked himself back and forth as though to comfort himself.

The weeping became slightly more desperate and he let out a whimper. He could break physical chains with his bare hands, but he could not break free from this invisible prison. A flash of lucidity came over him, a brief window, where he came to his senses. "God, help me, please ... help me! God please." He buried his head into his knees, but then *they* started. Day and night he was tormented by those voices that screamed in his head and sometimes spoke through his mouth. In this moment of stillness they seized the opportunity.

"Look at you, you're filth – you piece of garbage. You're nothing. We own you, we're all you have. Nobody wants you, nobody loves you. One day you'll throw your worthless carcass over a cliff and everyone will be happy you've gone."

He clamped his hands over his ears in a vain attempt to muffle the tirade. He stood up and now observed his naked form reflected back at him.

Mocking laughter lashed him and in a fit of anger he jumped on his reflection again and again. He punched and kicked the water as self-hatred boiled within. A bird startled by the sudden frenzy darted, squawking into the darkness.

Clouds invaded the clear night sky like the cursing crowds that often gathered to throw stones. The moon's brightness was snuffed out without ceremony and a storm angrily gripped and shook the lake, causing boats to be tossed about like corks.

The rain pelted and the wind roared and he, who had climbed to higher ground, just sat, staring, blank. He dragged sharp stones over the skin of his forearms over and over, first one and then the other. As the blood appeared, the rain diluted its rich redness to strawberry pink before it ran off his arms and mingled with the mud-splashed earth. His face expressed a strange mixture of pain and relief.

Strange that the storm died down as quickly as it had appeared. Peace and stillness had melted its ferocity and it flopped and fell into nothingness. Curling into the foetal position he slept a deep sleep.

The sky was already blue and cloudless when he awoke. Wincing as he moved, he looked at his raw arms with the blood of the night's activity baked hard in the early morning sun. Movement in the distance drew his eyes to some men pulling a boat up on the shore.

There was one man amongst them off whom he could not take his eyes. When he tried to move he seemed rooted to the spot, as though caught in the dream where he tries to run away but his legs won't work.

*"Get away! Don't go down there ... get away ... **run!**"* The voices unleashed their greatest fury ever.

Nausea and dizziness suddenly swept over him. The impulse to get away was almost overwhelming, but he could not take his eyes off *that Man*. He didn't know why. He just knew that he had to get to Him. The voices were as insistent as ever (*Get as far away as possible, he'll destroy us! You have to go. **Right now!**). Despite them, today it felt like he did not have to obey.

He squinted, seeking to maintain his focus and still he felt terrible. It was as though every ounce of energy had drained from his body. There was massive temptation (*That's right, you can do it*) to back off. Maybe then they would leave him alone.

He turned around and started to walk in the opposite direction and indeed, there was a kind of relief that came over him. Yet at the same time it felt so wrong. What was right? What was wrong? It had become almost impossible for him to discern insanity from sanity. In a moment he whipped around and began to run, trying to get as near to the shore as he could before anything stopped him. He made it.

As he arrived at the One whom he'd seen from a distance, he was compelled to bow. The tormentors within him could not stand upright in the presence of the One on the shore. Everyone was startled except the One whom they called Jesus, who, it seemed to the ever curious onlookers, was expecting him. As he looked into Jesus' face, he heard voices speak from his mouth, before he passed out.

"Wake up, My friend, wake up!" Jesus said. His gentle, but slightly rough hand brushed dirt from the man's confused face.

The moment was disturbed by a thunderous sound which made them both look up. There, just along the way, a large herd of pigs stampeded down the hillside and at full tilt charged into the lake. The thunder of trotters and squeals dissolved into silence except for the lapping waves of the water, which had been disturbed.

The man, wide-eyed, looked again into the eyes of Jesus. Jesus was smiling. He let out a slight chuckle,

"It's ok, it's over now – go wash and we'll sort you out with some clothes."

Suddenly aware of the filth and his nakedness, the man felt embarrassed and yet at the same time knew that he didn't need to be. The voices had gone and peace had taken up residence. For the first time in a long time, he actually wanted to live rather than wishing he was dead. Depression had dispersed. There was something about being near Jesus that left him feeling that there was purpose to his existence. He was actually worth something. Now that he'd found Him, he was totally convinced that he never wanted to leave the presence of this extraordinary Man.

Once washed and dressed, he sat at Jesus' feet hanging on His every word – this Man had done what no other could have. Little by little a crowd gathered and began slowly, tentatively, edging in towards him. This was a familiar scene, but this time it was different. Amazed and perplexed, they could see that the man they recognised was changed and they knew it! He was sure that they would be as enamoured with Jesus as he was. For if Jesus could help a depraved wretch such as he, then there was surely hope for them and their families.

It was difficult to make out what they were saying at first, but when he eventually caught it, he couldn't believe his own ears. They were begging Jesus to leave. They eventually became so insistent that, with a sigh, Jesus arose and made towards the boat with the other men who had travelled with Him.

The man who'd been set free followed to leave with Jesus. After all, why would he want to stay here?

Jesus stopped him.

"I know you want to come, My friend," Jesus said, "but your family (*He paused to look at the fearful faces huddling in the background*) and these people need you and need to know about Me. Go and tell them and everyone you meet about the good things God has done."

Jesus watched as disappointment flooded into the man's eyes. He winked and smiled. He couldn't help but awkwardly smile back.

He did go back to his family, but not before stopping off in all ten towns of the district to tell them of the day he met the Man on the shores of the Sea of Galilee and of all that God had done!

Far from being offended, I think the enemy likes the fact that we've taken his very real world and repackaged it in a sugar-coated, trick-or-treat one of funny hats, fairy tales and fantasy. He can continue his covert operations behind the cover that so many of us have given him.

Whilst it may seem at first more appropriate to take a cynical, it's fanciful unscientific, bury-your-head-in-the-sand approach, it is a dangerous stance to take. If we fail to recognise the enemy whilst he walks among us, we can find ourselves with a Trojan horse full of trouble that can take us out, while we're still wondering what happened. The enemy is real and can do real damage to real people. There is a power in the earth that is dedicated to destroying humanity and God's plan for our wellbeing.

We meet a man in this account who anyone would agree should have been certified. After all he was clearly a danger to himself and to society. In reality we don't have enough information to diagnose the exact mental illness by precise category, or to know how he got into the mess, but what we do know is that his severe problem had alienated him from society and left him a tormented, self-abusing, frightening wretch who inhabited the unclean ground between the graveyard and the non-Jewish pig-rearing territory. It was easier to live amongst the dead than it was to live amongst the living.

The enemy is strategic in his plan to isolate people. He knows the more isolated they are, the more vulnerable they are. There are some who sit alone and give off a "radar signal" not to come near. They have bought into a lie that nobody cares and they dare the world to prove them wrong. They sabotage any bridge that some brave soul may seek to build to get to them. Eventually, through continued rejection, people stop trying to build and then, with an almost perverted smug satisfaction, they gather yet more dubious evidence that nobody cares about them. People do not get to *this* place by themselves. They are survivors of adverse circumstances, their interpretations of their own worth and lack of value then leads them to be unwittingly wooed and cosseted by dark forces, working to a plan of isolation and annihilation.

We see in this story someone who hurts himself. It might be extremely difficult for many people to imagine or to comprehend, that someone's internal pain can be of such magnitude that inflicting physical pain on oneself can bring relief, albeit temporary. Of course, the soreness and shame follow, but at the time that seems a small price to pay. Intellectually, people who self-abuse would usually agree that it's not right and they wish they could stop and they even did for a while once, but ...

How horrendous it is to be in *that* much pain that for a moment (no matter how brief) it is a relief to hurt yourself. For most the road back from here is a challenging and difficult one that requires much help and counsel. But there is real hope that if Jesus can help to stop the pain on the inside, there's a possibility that He can also help you to deal with the urge to keep hurting yourself on the outside.

In the first book of the Bible, Genesis, there is the account of two brothers, Cain and Abel. In a jealous rage, Cain had killed Abel and God tells us that Abel's blood cried out to Him from the ground. I believe, in a similar way, that as this man abused himself and the blood dripped onto the ground, God heard his cry and sent a rescuer.

I want to encourage you that God has heard your cry. You may not have been able to verbalise it, but God heard and He will always make sure that, somehow, He will get the Rescuer to you.

At some point you will have a choice to run away from, or run to, the One who shed *His* blood, so that you wouldn't have to shed yours.

This man represents in many ways the plans that our vile enemy has for our lives. He had walked with demons that had controlled his mind and given him strength to break chains with his bare hands, but as per the enemy's master plan, he was running out of the strength to go on. Hidden not too well amongst those chilling screams was a cry that came before the throne of God ... the cry of a man who longed to be free. I believe Jesus was on a mission that day to answer that cry!

We are faced here with three great powers. The bondage-making power of an enemy, the bondage-breaking power of God and the sustaining power of the human will.

For the record, I believe it is possible that someone, be they Christian or not, can be inhabited with supernatural influences called demons. I can already hear the dissenting voices crying out, but it's not the purpose of this book to answer those questions. I'm here for those who know that they've tried so hard but to no avail. They've tried self-control, prayer, fasting, retreats, confessing and applying the word of God and yet *still* they battle to the point of exhaustion in certain areas. I believe that we should be open to the fact that Jesus told us to cast out demons for a reason. Dealing with the demonic does not rid us of the responsibility for self-control, nor does it stop us having to take every thought captive and make it submit to Christ[1] as well as taking appropriate biblical precautions to stop us falling into sin. But what it does do is deal with the gravitational pull towards failure.

Have you ever seen those strength tests where people have super strong elastic secured to their backs and have to run to retrieve things? At first it's easy to run against what's pulling them back, but the longer they do it, the more tired they become, the more they lose the strength to fight the force that is pulling them back. In dealing with the demonic, Jesus snips the elastic (as it were) that keeps pulling you back. You still have to run, but you find a new ability to stop going back to the place you used to go.

This man's life had been at the extreme end of this vicious circle and had been powerfully ravaged by demonic power, but as powerful as it was, it was not powerful enough to resist two things. The obvious one is the power of God through the spoken words of Jesus, but maybe the less obvious one, is the power of the human will.

I put it to you that this man, through the power of the will, had managed to get to Jesus when every demon within him would have been screaming "stay away". He ran with all his strength against the pull of the elastic!

Secondly, I think that what those demons did to the pigs, they'd been trying to do to the man all along. The pigs didn't have the will to resist, but this man had been running against the pull of the elastic for a long time. In this regard I like to think that Jesus and His disciples had got to him in the nick of time. They'd been hindered by a demonically instigated storm that they had met as they journeyed to the region, but the devil could not stop what God had started.

Strength to keep running against the pull was ebbing. The enemy had tried to take this life before he could meet with the Rescuer, but he failed. This represents great hope that, no matter how bad things in your life may be – *and* you may even be out of your mind, driven by demonic powers, deep within you is the God-given will, the ability to choose whether to get to the Rescuer or not. You *can* choose, you *can* decide to break free, to move on, to stay, to stop, to live, to be what you were born to be. You are not helpless or hopeless. Get up and run again. The pull back may be very strong, but get up and run to Him.

You may be desperate and lonely, perhaps viewing (as this man did) Jesus from a distance. You, too, may be faced with the challenge to run away or run to Him. He who has the power to set you free is waiting for you.

The Crazy Man was found "clothed and in his right mind"[2] at the feet of Jesus. He had been released *from* his torment and released *to* the special task that Jesus asked him to do. Once he had been the man the devil used to influence a region, he was the man that God was using now.

Some of this man's issues may (or may not be) your issues. The point is, no matter how powerfully overwhelming your circumstances may be, no matter how painful, Jesus is able to release you from your torment and into your destiny. He is waiting for you "on the shore" – which way will you run?

Notes

1. 2 Corinthians 10:5.
2. Mark 5:15.

CHAPTER 5

BLIND FAITH
(Mark 10:46–52)

Even before the first light of dawn the guards dragged their sticks across the bars, as they did every day, to wake the prisoners. Not that there was any purpose in them waking so early, it was just prison routine. This was my first time here or, in fact, in any prison. I was caught stealing my master's chickens and selling them at market. Though I begged for mercy, he was having none of it. He wanted to make an example of me and so here I am.

I wiped the sleep from my eyes and realised how much I stank; not that it mattered much, because everybody stank. The cell was dimly lit by the guard's oil lamp that sat on the table just on the other side of the bars and produced enough light for me to gaze at the bemused and pitiful assortment of humanity that kept me company. There was one small slit of a window, which was our only source of ventilation and natural light and was adequate for neither.

I didn't know what the old man in the corner was in for, but it must have been bad, because he was chained day and night. Over the last few weeks I'd noticed that each morning he went through a strange ritual. He would slowly, as if in considerable pain, inch his way forward until his chains were strained to the maximum and were bruising and biting into his flesh. There he sat, staring, through the window. Every day at the same time, just before sunrise, as the rest of us were barely awake.

He was gaunt and pale, with the sort of paleness that comes from your skin not seeing the sun for a long time. His face was etched with the deep lines that only many years can bring. His lips were cracked and dry and his hair hung wispy, white and wild. Funny, I had noticed before, but now I noticed again that his eyes ... there was something about those eyes. Though framed in this tired old face, they were so clear and kind and seemed to tell a story. Nobody talked to him, because the guards forbade it. I guessed he must be crazy, because I often looked across and saw his lips moving and yet they made no sound.

This place was a hell hole. Our long nights were tormented by fleas, rats and the crazed screams of my fellow inmates' troubled sleep. Our days were tortured with the boredom of excruciating nothingness. But the old man in the corner seemed remarkably untouched by it all. Here I was having trouble surviving the few weeks I'd been here and he'd been here forever. *Maybe that's the best way to endure this ... to slip quietly into insanity*, I thought.

But then if that's the case, why did I feel the need so strongly to talk to him?

I mean, why was I so fascinated by this crazy old guy? And why did the guards work so hard at keeping everyone away from him? Anyone caught trying to speak to him would be beaten (and I wasn't sure that I wanted to speak to him so much that I'd risk a beating).

Once a week the guard change took longer than usual. On a Thursday there was always a fresh batch of prisoners and for some reason sorting all that out took all the guards and kept them away for longer than usual. That was going to be my moment of opportunity.

Well, I was beginning to wonder if I had got the right day, but it was just that the fresh intake was late and I heard a couple of guards saying its because it was larger than usual. This was good news ... it would mean that it would take longer to sort out.

The last guard glanced back as he left, perhaps he'd forgotten something, and finally we were alone, for a little while at least. I slipped to other side of the cell where it seemed the old man was sleeping. The guard came back unexpectedly, to collect some keys when suddenly one of the prisoners screamed, making the guard jump.

"Be quiet, you crazy old fool!" came the guard's retort, but he left again in a hurry without noticing I'd moved. I'm surprised he hadn't heard my heart pounding in my chest. My eyes closed with relief.

"Fear is the greatest prison of all." The voice was clear. I turned to see from where it had come. It was the old man, who I thought was asleep, watching me.

"I'm sorry?" It wasn't that I hadn't heard, but it was just that I wanted to see him say it!

He swallowed and repeated himself.

"Fear – it's the greatest prison of all!" He coughed weakly from the exertion of raising the volume.

"I'm not afraid," I said.

"You should be," the old man replied. "You should be afraid that you are in here wasting the precious life that God has given you."

"God?" I replied, "I think He gave up on me long ago."

Suddenly the old man was more animated and alert than I had ever seen him and when he spoke, he seemed agitated.

"Never say that!" he said.

"What?" I replied.

"That God has given up on you. He *never* gives up on you."

"How come you're so sure of that?" I asked, "I mean . . . you're here, aren't you?"

The old man actually laughed. "You do have a point there!" But becoming serious again in an instant he said,

"But God *has* never and *will* never give up on me." He half lifted his chain bound hand for emphasis.

"Why are you here, old man? You must be a murderer, or a rebel or . . . "

"Steady on, son, I'm none of those things. I'm here because I followed a man."

"What? Is He here as well?" I inquired, looking around the cell.

"No, He died a long time ago"

I didn't say anything, but I knew I looked confused.

"To understand the end of a matter, one must be familiar with the beginning," he said. The confusion didn't budge!

"When I was a child, I was afflicted with an illness that eventually left me completely blind."

"No way!" I said, "Now you're just having me on. You're not blind."

"Do you want to know or don't you?" the old man said and promptly had another coughing fit.

"Ok, ok," I said, "you were blind . . . "

"Completely," said the old man. "My parents put me out to beg from a young age and this was basically how I grew up, baking in the sun and eating the dust that was kicked up around me by passers-by. All I longed for was to hear a coin or two being placed on the cloak that lay before me. I had lived in a world of darkness for so long that I could hardly remember that I'd seen any light at all. Hazy images hung around in my memories and invaded my dreams, but with the passing of time, they just got hazier and the darkness began to close in. I was afraid of that . . . that past and present would just merge and all light would be driven away forever. To think that this was all there was to life was almost unbearable. My eyes may have been dim, but my hearing was as sharp as ever and one day I heard word of a man called Jesus and that He was a healer."

"Was he a magician?" I asked.

"No," said the old man. "We had been taught that One would come, a Son of David, and that He would heal. When I heard about the things people said He had done, I believed that He could heal me and that I needed to get to Him."

The old man turned to look at me directly and with passion in his eyes he asked, "Have you ever been desperate?"

"What ... desperate like I'm desperate to get out of here?" I replied a little glibly.

"Yes, sort of," he said "Except I was desperate to get out of a different prison. My only escape was a miracle."

"I think my only escape is a miracle," I said.

"Well, God is a God of miracles," the old man said. "One day as I sat in my usual spot, I heard an unusual sort of commotion and so I called out, 'What's happening?' They told me that Jesus the Nazarene was about to pass by. 'Jesus the Nazarene,' I said to myself. 'That's Him! Jesus the healer!' Without a thought, I began to shout at the top of my voice,

Jesus, Son of David, have mercy on me!

The crowd, irritated by the noise, began ordering me to be quiet. But I was being quiet for nobody. If my healer was about to pass by, I wasn't going to miss my opportunity. So when they yelled at me to shut me up, I yelled even more frantically, until I almost had no voice left. They were not going to stop me getting to Jesus. Then they stopped yelling and said, 'He's calling you, go on, He's calling.' And then I felt hands grip me and lift me up and guide me to Jesus.

'What do you want Me to do for you?' A voice I'd never heard before hit me like a lightning strike.

'Lord', I said, 'I want to see.'

'Alright, your faith has healed you.'

Instinctively I opened my eyes – and I could see!"

"What . . . just like that?" I said, but the old man didn't reply because he was weeping and moving his lips without making a noise again, but I did hear a "Thank You, God," just before he responded to me with,

"Just like that! I was blind and then I could see."

"What was the first thing you saw?" I asked.

"Him!" came the reply.

"It was incredible. He was incredible. The moment was incredible. For years I've wanted to live it again and again, but the closest thing I've ever found to *that* moment was when the sun rises."

And suddenly I got it, "And that's why you shuffle around every morning . . ."

"To see a glimpse," the old man interrupted, "a slither of that glorious moment, when darkness was gone and I could see."

"And then what happened?" I asked.

"Well, I followed Him of course, right until the end."

"The end?"

"They crucified Him. The most wonderful man who ever walked the face of the earth, they killed Him."

"You must have been devastated," I said.

"We were."

"We?" I asked.

"Yes, those who followed with me, until we understood that it had to be and He'd been trying to tell us about it all along! He died to set you and me free."

"Me?" I exclaimed, "How did I get involved in all this?"

"You are very much involved, because Jesus wants to open your eyes too," he replied.

"But I'm not blind," I said.

"You have sight, but you can't see how much He loves you . . .

how much He's done for you . . . how much He's got for you," he replied. His words struck me again and again and I was confused as to why I was so affected by them. A silence that was beginning to feel uncomfortable had developed. I didn't know what to say and then I remembered my question, so I asked,

"And so why are you in here?"

"For telling my story, for telling people about what Jesus has done. I could tell you hundreds of stories about what He's done for other people, not just for me."

"That's it?" I said, "You've been chained up and left to rot for that?"

"It's a powerful message," said the old man, "with the potential to change individuals, communities and nations."

"And *that's* why they've locked you up and won't let you talk to anybody . . . to stop your story, this message," I said.

"Oh, they'll never stop it," he grinned, "when one door closes another will open."

I didn't understand what he meant, but I didn't have the heart to ask him. He looked tired and yet radiant in a strange sort of way. As I began to shuffle back to my place, I said finally, "I wish I could have met Him . . . Jesus."

The man laughed. "Oh, you can, you can, you only have to ask and He'll come right into your heart!"

It was just the worst moment for the guards to return. I wanted to know what he meant, but it was too late. I sat and watched him all day, moving his lips and making no sound, until the light was too faded to see anymore. I sat in the darkness and thought about all that had been said and I knew that I wanted it, but I was scared.

The old man's words echoed in my head, "You only have to ask and He'll come right into your heart." So I did.

✛   ✛   ✛

The stick made its usual rattling journey somewhere between a ping and a thud along the bars, but this morning I was looking forward with excitement to finding an opportunity to talk with the old man and to let him know somehow what I'd done. He was still asleep, though I knew that I only had to wait for sunrise. But with the first gleam of dawn, he didn't move. He remained slumped in the corner. I knew instantly that something was wrong and shouted for the guard.

"Old man?" the guard called across to him. There was no response, so he increased the volume: "Bartimaeus?"

I was so surprised. They never spoke to him like that. They never called him by name. I was willing him to move, but there was nothing. The guard reluctantly came into the cell and poked the old man with his foot, then held the back of his hand near his nose and mouth.

"He's a goner," he said to no one in particular and left him.

I couldn't believe it. How could this happen? I suddenly felt horribly alone, cheated even. Two guards returned with a stretcher and I watched them unchain the old man and lay him unceremoniously upon it. I couldn't help but notice how peaceful he looked in the full morning light.

Unexpectedly, a third guard came in and called my name. I indicated it was me and he said abruptly,

"Follow me!"

"Why? Where are we going?" I asked.

"All charges have been dropped, you're free to go," he said, clearly irritated by me requiring more information.

I didn't let my confusion bring out any further questions. I just followed.

The old man, Bartimaeus, left on the stretcher just before me. In my head I heard his voice say clearly again, "Oh, they'll never stop it; when one door closes another opens."

They may have tried to stop him telling *his* story, but now

I would tell it! I'd tell our stories of a miracle working God . . .
One who opens blind eyes and sets the prisoner free!

My mother used to say many things and not all of them
repeatable. However, one of the phrases she often used was,
"There's none as blind as those who do not want to see," and
though I don't know where she got it from, I know it's true.

If you are determined not to see, then you won't.

Helen Keller[1] spoke of the tragedy of having sight, but no
vision.

The Bible tells us that *"people without a vision or revelation
cast off restraint."*[2] People without a vision for their life tend to
live carelessly.

Jesus told us, in fact commanded us, to love our neighbour as
ourselves, but maybe we do and *that's* part of the problem. We
despise and abuse others, because we despise and abuse
ourselves and we despise and abuse ourselves because we don't
know what the purpose of our life is. If we have no purpose we
have no value and it's much easier to abuse that which we do not
value. If you consider your existence to be cheap and plastic then
it also becomes entirely disposable.

I don't think that that's the only reason we pour in stuff, inject
. . . sniff and use sex to sedate ourselves. I think we do these
things to ease the pain, because we look down the long dark
tunnel of life and think, "What's the point? So many things can go
wrong . . . let's just live for the moment."

I don't know how you arrived on planet earth, whether you
were born to loving parents or abusive ones. Whether you were
wanted or not wanted. Maybe you were the product of a rape or
don't even know who your real parents are, but here you are!

As the old man said, "If one wants to understand the end of a
matter one must be familiar with the beginning." The Bible says,

"God saw you being formed in your mother's womb,"[3] and that, *"all the days ordained for you were written in* [His] *book before one of them came to be,"*[4] which means that you were not just the result of a sperm meeting an egg. God planned your existence. You are here for a purpose and if the landing was rough, then at least understand that, with God, it is not how you start it is how you finish!

How many of us waste our time, wishing we were this person or that person? That we were taller, faster, blonder or whatever, and fail to realise that we arrived equipped for the purpose for which God brought us into this world. If we want to see, then we will see that God planned us because God wanted us here and if we are not an accident of biology, then we have a purpose and if we have a purpose, then life is far from pointless, because we each have the responsibility to release our ability. It's God-given ... unique and necessary.

"Great!" I hear you say, "I accept I'm a person of purpose with the responsibility to release my ability ... but what is my ability?"

Uh oh there is a *slight* catch!

The first step is to realise that there actually is treasure there. But it's buried. To unearth that treasure will take determination and time (and possibly a strategically placed stick of dynamite), but it is there and God is more determined to get it out than you are. No doubt the journey is tough in parts, but it's a journey that God never wanted you to take alone. He always intended coming along, if you want Him, that is. (Just to make the additional point in favour of having Him along) He knows what the treasure is and where it is. He knows because *He* put it there – He doesn't just know the map, He *is* the map!

"Ok, fine, but if God knows what it is and where it is, why for heaven's sake does He not just show us?"

The answer is simple, if not popular – "Because He loves us

too much." Remember, we've already talked about the fact that God is more concerned about the end than the beginning.

Well there is such a thing as preparation: When our third child, Joseph, was born, my wife in her wisdom used to feed him dehydrated food. In those days it was all the rage. You picked a box with glorious pictures of delicious carrots, potatoes and *green*, green peas, poured boiling water on the flakes you'd poured out of the box and produced a vile sludge that bore no resemblance to the picture on the box. And we believed that it was good for our baby ... *what on earth were we thinking?*

On one particular day, Joseph was screaming (with copious amounts of snot and tears for effect), because he wanted his sludge. He wanted it, I was desperate for him to have it (anything to stop the racket), and his mother was taking too long for both of us!

His mother was vigorously stirring and blowing, trying to cool down the food and make it ready to eat.

Joseph could see it, smell it, and almost taste it (so could I, but I didn't want to taste it!). The truth was, if he'd had it when he wanted it ... instead of doing him good, it would have burned and harmed him.

Sometimes we get frustrated with God, because He seems to be taking too long with what *we* want and so we scream and shout and complain. But if we are mature we will realise that there is not only a right *thing*, but a right *time*.

God is not a cruel tease, but needs us to understand that in the process of excavating the treasure, He is also preparing the vessel in which He will display it.

Often life is about choices and we have to choose to see. Choose to see that you are here for a purpose and that there *is* a plan for your life. Choose to see that whether others have caused you to stumble or you have tripped yourself up ... if God is *for* you then who can be against you?[5] Choose to see that God will never

be hindered by circumstances and with Him nothing is impossible![6] Choose to see, even though there may only be enough light
for the next step, take that step! If God says there is a path ...
there is!

Faith, actually, is never "blind". It will always choose to see
God's possibilities and believes that as one door closes another
will open. Following Jesus leads to the kind of freedom that can
never be imprisoned.

Is it not time to open your eyes and choose to see?

Notes

1. Keller, Helen,
        www.brainyquote.com/quotes/authors/h/helen_keller.html.
2. Proverbs 29:18: compare the King James Version and New International
    Version
3. Jeremiah 1:5.
4. Psalm 139:16.
5. Romans 8:31.
6. Luke 1:37.

CHAPTER 6

THE BIG ISSUE
(Mark 5:21–34)

She could not bring herself to look them in the eye. She didn't want to see that look she'd seen so often in the last five years. Her body ached, and her soul ached even more to hear good news; so many opinions, so much money, so many vile lotions and potions and so much disappointment. The truth is she hadn't got better, she'd grown worse, much worse.

The three doctors returned to the table after conferring in hushed tones on the other side of the room. One didn't really speak at all, the other seemed gentle and caring and the third was agitated and bullish in comparison to his colleagues. It was he who spoke.

"There is nothing more we can do," he blurted, "I'm sorry – your payment is due."

He was then the first to move away, soon followed by the quiet one. She lifted her eyes in order to catch the gaze of the one doctor who might show some compassion, but his eyes were fixed on the cloth, frayed at the edges, dampened with sweat and clutched in her slightly trembling hands. It enshrouded the last of her money and her fingers wouldn't work properly to open it. Without shifting his gaze, he said,

"May I?"

He took it from her, released the money and draped the cloth back over her hands, which had remained in "freeze frame". He half smiled his thanks and left.

She would have sat there for a long time, but another member of staff opened the door to indicate it was time to leave. She understood. For a moment, outside, she found herself over-whelmed by the din and bustle of a day that was drawing to a close. She tried to walk, but her legs wouldn't seem to work properly. She felt faint, and with her head in a spin, she propped herself against a wall.

The amber and red hues of the dying day bathed all before her in beauty. The dust, dense in parts, danced and swirled in the golden light before caking the back of her throat.

A woman gracefully picked her way across the busy street. Briefly, the other woman caught her eye and changed direction. Years ago she herself had been like that, strong, confident and beautiful, she remembered. Now, battered and faded by sickness, she could hardly recognise the person she had become.

She recalled the day she realised that her period was lasting longer than it usually did. She thought nothing of it at first, but month by month the flow increased, until she bled more days than not. Twelve years of bleeding. Treatments had taken their toll; friends and family had fallen away, believing her to be cursed by God. Surely she must have done something terrible for this to have continued so long. Unclean, she could not mix publicly and loneliness clawed its way in leaving a void where belonging had once lived.

Her life was slowly draining away and all she kept hearing was, "There is nothing I can do for you. There's nothing that anyone could do." Why couldn't she just accept it? It really would be so much simpler. This was the question that she would not answer. White knuckles had wrapped themselves around hope and would not let go. The relentless echo that bounced around her hollow soul cried out night and day, "I am worth more than this!"

"Look, Mummy! That woman is bleeding."

Snapped back to reality, she looked and saw horror on a child's face, then down to see that a small pool of blood had developed at her feet. In that moment it seemed that all eyes were turned to look accusingly at her. Hurriedly she kicked dirt over it and scurried home to change and to escape the looks of disgust.

Her chest rose and fell as she leaned against the door she had slammed shut, exhausted by exertion. She soaked up the safety she felt from the tiny room she now called home.

She washed, changed and sat down. She watched the candle flame dance and die, snuffed out by a sudden wind, leaving her in total darkness. Gradually her attention was drawn to the fact that the wind had also parted the clouds to reveal the moon, bright and full. Its light not only invaded the room, but seemed to penetrate her very soul. It was almost as though she was supposed to understand some underlying significance.

And then, there it was again – that unreasonable, overwhelming sense that somehow all would be well. How could she dare to hope that anything would ever be different? Why could she not just accept what the doctors told her? Despite herself, she stood up with anticipation. She had to pace because she did not know what else to do with the torrent of emotions that welled up from within. She could not hear an audible voice, but somewhere, at her epicentre, there was something that called out to her, which she strained to hear, yet it was all to no avail. Eventually she lay down, eyes heavy, and slept until another day was well underway.

She had woken with something on her mind ... well, someone to be more precise. There was this God-man, the son of a carpenter from Nazareth, of whom everyone was talking. Definitely mixed reviews, but she heard that people were healed at His touch and there were even crazy rumours around that He had raised the dead.

Some even said He might be the Messiah! She found that her mind was making strange links. The moonlight of the previous night reminded her of an obscure verse from the great prophet Isaiah, who had spoken of a day when the moon would be as bright as the sun and that this would be a sign that the Lord would begin to heal His people and cure them of their wounds. If He was who He said He was, was it possible that somehow God could . . . would heal her?

She knew she had to find Him and she rushed out of the door with a strength that was not her own. Not knowing where to go or which way to turn, it then occurred to her to go towards the synagogue. Even if He wasn't there, then maybe there would be someone who could point her in the right direction.

As the synagogue came in to view, she noticed the crowd gathered outside and there was a man on his knees, talking to someone.

As she drew closer, she realised that the man kneeling was the leader of the synagogue. People were amazed and some wondered why he, being who he was, should kneel before this carpenter's son. Maybe, like her, desperation made him see with the eyes of the soul.

In a flash, the strength that had carried her here abandoned her. Faltering, she found herself overwhelmed with her uncleanness. All her experience told her she had no right to be here. She should have turned back, not to allow herself to pollute anyone, but couldn't. She knew that to touch a Rabbi was to take her life into her hands. But she had watched her options bleed away. What did she have to lose, her reputation? That had gone long ago! Her life? That was as good as over anyway. She had to get to this God-man. If He had something that she could have then she was going to reach out and take it. He didn't know her, He hadn't come to see her, but she refused to let this opportunity pass her by and besides, with all these people around, who would notice her?

In a moment, the man who had been kneeling was up on his feet and urging Jesus to follow him. Both He and the crowd began to move and she kept losing sight of Him, but she said to herself over and over,

"If I can just touch the edge of His robe then I will be well."

People pressed all around Him, but all the while they were looking at Him, they were not noticing her. She kept trying to reach through the crowd, but it seemed her arms were too short. Moving up, falling back, moving up and falling back. The tears of frustration burned her eyes, but determination burned in her soul. Her strength, though, was failing her. She wasn't able to keep this up and then, almost at the point of giving up, someone stumbled into her, giving her the momentum to reach and touch.

Immediately everything stopped. Something like lightning shot through her that knocked her back and held her up all at the same time. She was elated. She had done it. She knew that something had reached within and made her well, but elation soon turned to fear as she heard Him say,

"Who touched Me?"

His voice instantly reminded her of the one she had strained to hear deep within. Hearing it brought clarity and peace, the placing of the final piece of the jigsaw.

The crowd gasped and muttered amongst themselves. Some men began to challenge the God-man; it was obvious to them that with the crowd pressing in around Him He was being bumped into all the time.

"Somebody touched me. I felt power leave." [1]

Feeling extremely conspicuous she wanted to run and hide, but as a thousand eyes scanned the crowd, she knew there was no escape.

In a moment it seemed that all those eyes locked on to her. People drew back as they realised that an unclean one was amongst them. Some even voiced their disgust. What was she to do? Without thinking, she threw herself at the feet of the God-man, trembling uncontrollably as power, excitement, gratitude and fear pulsated round her frail frame. She couldn't bring herself to look at Him, but she found the strength to say through her tears,

"Master, forgive me! In the twelve years I've been ill I paid so many doctors that I've lost everything. When I heard about You, I just believed that You, being who You are, could make me well, so I said to myself 'just touch the hem of His coat.'"

She slowly lifted her head to look at Him, but the sun was behind Him and the brightness made her squint and look to one side.

There was a slight pause before He said,

"Your faith has made you well."

Dizzy with an intoxicating mixture of relief and delight, she rose to her feet and stood before Him. For the first time she looked into His eyes and her soul was set on fire by the intensity of the love she found there.

She noticed that she was standing a little taller and felt strong in a way that she couldn't remember and, as if knowing her thoughts, a smile broke out on His face as they shared that moment together. And then, like a cloud blocking the sun, the crowd closed in again and moved on.

Rooted to the spot once more, she toyed with the idea of following, but she instinctively knew it wasn't necessary. Her grey world had burst into magnificent colour. It was indeed a beautiful day and time to go home and change!

It's not easy to pick yourself up when you've gone ten rounds in the ring with disappointment and you're down. It's certainly not comfortable to watch. Those who can't bear it will want you to

throw in the towel. They will seek to convince you that it's for your own good, as they take their own discomfort and heavily disguise it as compassion.

You get up again, not because you love being hit, but because you have the audacity to believe that you can not only stand, but win!

This is the unreasonableness of faith. Once it has taken you hostage there can be no negotiations: it's do or die! Twelve minutes can seem a long time if you are waiting for a bus in the rain, so waiting for your miracle for twelve years is an eternity in comparison.

In all that time, it's not so easy to shut out the voices in the crowd when they agree with the dark and sinister voices within. But somehow we have to stoop and pick up that torch of hope, shine it down the tunnel of our despair and just keep walking. We keep on fanning the flames of our expectation because, if *that* fire goes out, we really are finished!

Hope and expectation support us when the crowd have gone home embarrassed, shaking their heads as they go. Defying convention, these warriors will guide us through hostile territory to our miracle. We have to listen for and pay attention to the voices, external and/or internal that scream support from the sidelines and tell us what we need to hear in order to get us out of bed in the morning!

Remember, she was saying to herself,

"If I can just..."

The voice of the inner coach can steer us to, or away from, our divine appointment. What kind of tape is playing in your head all day? Do you curse yourself when you make a mistake? Does that voice continually undermine you? Are you ensnared by letting what plays in your head spill out of your mouth? Only you can press stop and start, playing stuff that's worth listening to. When our words won't work, God's will!

We thank God for His sustaining grace. We wouldn't have made it this far without it and we'd have lost our way or lost our mind. That grace will keep us until we are in the position to run away or reach out and touch ... it's your call.

There are many lessons to learn from this account:

It's not over until God says it's over! The tenacity that drove her to get mended, until she was broke, positioned her to break through her doubts and fears and come to Jesus. This woman refused to curl up and die.

Her passion to be different caused her to ignore the religious conventions of the day and to reach out and take something that was not being offered to her. That's the funny thing about desperation – it forgets its manners and pushes and barges its way to the front and will not leave until it gets what it wants.

As for those tutting and pointing at this audacious behaviour, let's take a moment to remember that not only does Jesus appear to like it, it definitely gets results.

The crowd was close to Jesus, fascinated by Him, many actually touching Him and yet receiving nothing. The fact that this is possible is actually a scary thought – to be *that* close and miss it!

What stopped the God-man in His tracks was a touch that stood out from others. The star of our story believed that He *was* who He said He was and it's precisely *that* kind of belief that unlocked the treasure that everyone else missed.

Hunger also plays a big role here, a hunger for God, a hunger to be different! This kind of hunger will cause you to leap-frog the social norms, be oblivious to criticism and press in uninvited to receive the desire of your heart.

Have you waited a long time? You might not want to admit it, but you have, haven't you? Waited and believed, believed and waited. In fact, it's been so long, you've learned to put people off the scent of your pain by hiding behind a smile, or a lie, or whatever it is you hide behind.

Know this, you can't hide from God and I don't know why it's all taking so long, but His grace will keep you and position you to be in the right place at the right time. For those of you who think you've missed it and believe it's all too late – the devil is a liar! Get up and get to Jesus! No-one else can run your race for you, or touch Him for you. She knew within herself she had been made well. You will need to know for yourself too. It's scary to risk disappointment all over again, but here's the thing – what's worse, to die wondering or die trying? In the end, we all realise, it's not what we get from Him that is the prize – He *is* the prize!

Don't you dare curl up and die! While there is life in your body, you pursue Him! Hang on, hold on, get up and press in . . . you are worth more than this! There may be all kinds of obstacles between you and Him, but keep going because the God-man has your miracle!

Notes _____

1. Luke 8:46.

CHAPTER 7

UNTOUCHABLE
(Luke 5:12–14)

Rachel arched her back, seeking to bring some relief to the strained and aching muscles. Supporting them with one hand and wiping her brow with the other, she blew hard to release the strand of hair that clung to her cheek, but it didn't budge. It was a scorcher. She bent over again and continued to fill the basket with the rocks that might damage her plough. She thought she'd seen something out of the corner of her eye, but thinking it was a rabbit, she'd just carried on, but now curiosity got the better of her. Standing to her full height, she squinted through the waves of heat that rose towards the cloudless sky.

They didn't get visitors anymore, so when she noticed it was *someone* and not something, she was more than surprised. Puffs of dust rose with each step that seemed to be getting faster. Even though the sun was directly in her line of vision, she could tell it was a man and immediately fear seized her heart in its icy grip.

Straightaway, she wanted to turn and run towards the house, which she was about to do, but for some reason she remained rooted to the spot. All she could make out was his long and unkempt hair, wild beard and clothes that were nothing more than rags. She really should run now, but there was something, something familiar, about the way he walked that held her attention. He was shouting something ... it sounded like her name. There it was again . . . it *was* her name. Her heart was pounding furiously now and her breathing became little more than a pant; she swallowed hard but her mouth was so dry it was a pointless exercise. Lifting her hand to her brow to shield her eyes from the sun, she moved a few tentative steps forward to improve her view.

If she didn't know better she would have sworn it was . . . but it couldn't be . . . how could it be? "My God . . . Josiah?" spilled out of her quivering lips.

"Josiiiiaaah!" she yelled as she ran at full pelt towards him, all hesitancy having completely abandoned her. He was now running too. Just before reaching him, she stopped dead in her tracks and he followed suit. Neither uttered a word as they eyed each other. Dust hung like smoke in the air and began to settle on their perspiration covered faces.

Disbelief engulfed her for a moment and she blinked as though this was no more than an apparition. He is too thin, she thought.

"It's me, Rachel," he said.

She gasped at the sound of his voice and slowly began to reach out to touch the lips that had spoken. Her trembling fingers and dirt filled nails made contact with his lips. In response, he lifted his hand to touch the side of her face tenderly. She quizzically touched his face back, running her fingers gently across the surface of his cheek, his nose. She took the hand cupping her cheek and examined it in the light as though seeing a hand for the very first time. Those lips spoke again. "It's gone." She looked deep into his eyes as though searching for reassurance.

"*All* gone!" Throwing herself into his waiting arms, she began to sob uncontrollably with wonder and relief. Tears flowed from both their eyes and they kissed and hugged.

Rachel, talking *to* him for the first time, then spoke, "I don't understand . . . where . . . how?" The ability to form proper sentences seemed to have evaded her. Josiah, understanding completely, replied, "Baby, God has given me a miracle. The priest has declared me clean; it's over."

Looking up the hill, thatch glinting in the sunlight, he saw the simple but beloved home he'd left so very long ago. They both wept *that* day too, but it was from a place of despair that neither had ever experienced before and would hope to never experience again. As they drew near to the house, suspicious children, a boy and a girl, came out.

"Dad!" the boy called and ran to greet Josiah who had dropped to one knee to meet him. The girl, who had been a baby when he'd left, had no recollection of the wild looking man she now saw before her. She ran straight past him to bury herself in her mother's skirt.

Rachel tried to dig her out and present her to her father, but she resisted and seeing slight agitation in Rachel, Josiah said reassuringly,

"It's ok ... leave her ... we've got time."

In a flash, as only children can, the boy swept the long absence away in an instant. "Come and look at the fire I've made," and ran ahead of them back to the house excitedly.

Both Josiah and Rachel admired his handiwork. "I will need to use it for a celebration supper," Rachel said. The boy's chest swelled with pride, erupting into a dance of joy. His sister joined in, enjoying the fun without understanding what it was all about.

"I've missed so much," Josiah said, looking sad for the first time.

Rachel touched his lips once again. "God will make it up to us, you'll see." A contagious smile broke out on her sun scorched face. "Let me fetch you some water."

Josiah did not want to let her out of his sight, but she slipped inside, returning with a clay beaker which Josiah emptied in a moment and then wiped his mouth with the back of his hand. He couldn't help but notice that Rachel was staring at him again. Realising she'd been caught, she immediately apologized, but continued to stare. "It's so difficult to take in, Josiah," she said.

Chores were put on hold for the day and they just enjoyed being in one another's company once again. It seemed ridiculous to be so shy with one another, but they giggled and blushed as they had in the days before they married. While Rachel cooked, Josiah cleaned up and put on some proper clothes to enjoy their celebration supper. It was a long time since he'd felt this good or eaten so well. Rachel cleared up and readied the children for bed and he, with a full stomach and pain free, allowed himself a moment of reflection.

It had all started with unexplained patches on his face, which at first gave no concern. Then one day, whilst moving a pot of boiling water, he splashed his hand without noticing as he tripped over a stone he did not feel with his foot. Before his eyes, he watched the blister begin to form on the now red, raw skin.

He tried to convince himself that this wasn't happening . . . that it wasn't as bad as it seemed. Eventually he hardly dared go into town anymore, because people were beginning to notice and comment. Then people began to keep their distance and he was forced to go to the priest. The priest sent him away for a week, then another one, allowing time for improvement, but there was none. Eventually he said those words that made Josiah sick to his stomach.

"I'm sorry, Josiah. I am compelled to declare you ceremonially unclean. Say good bye to your family and move out of the village before sunset."

As the sun began to dip in the sky, Rachel was crying almost hysterically as Josiah left. He couldn't even look back, his heart hurt so much. He thought he would die before he reached the bottom of the hill. He didn't, but there were many times in the days to come that he would wish he had. He dared a final glance at Rachel, his beloved Rachel, fervently rocking their small son, as she did when he cried; but he couldn't hear it crying, he was too far away, he thought. Even though he couldn't hear, he could see his son looking up to his mother in utter bewilderment.

"Josiah, the children are asleep now."

Startled back to reality by hearing his name, Josiah realised that he was still not used to hearing voices in close proximity. Rachel came to sit next to him, took his hand and wrapped hers around it. Neither of them could actually believe this was happening. They sat like this for a little while, just enjoying being close.

"What was it like, Josiah?"

Josiah winced at her question. Talking was something else he'd grown used to *not* doing. He wasn't sure he was ready yet as he watched the golden hues of the fire dance on her face as dusk settled in, but he found he couldn't refuse her.

Rubbing his head against her, as a pet dog might greet someone, Josiah said, "Well, I wasn't allowed to do anything like this, for a start." It was an attempt to be humorous, but they both knew it wasn't going to work. Rachel half-smiled and Josiah continued.

"Whenever I was walking and I accidentally came across people, I would have to cover my mouth and shout, 'Unclean! Unclean!' at the top of my voice. I felt so ashamed. Often people, panic struck, would scurry away as though to avoid some unpleasant insect. Some kind people would often leave scraps outside the village, but the dogs would usually get there first. There were one or two other lepers around but one was quite insane. I don't know whether he'd always been that way, or become that way. The other one had been alone so long, he'd become little more than an animal."

"You know?" Josiah paused, "Severe pain always tormented my body, but that was nothing compared to the excruciating loneliness and loss of dignity I felt. I just roamed aimless and in exile. I often thought of trying to come to see you and the family, but it was just too risky."

Rachel was weeping now. Josiah wanted to stop, because it was upsetting her, but after blowing her nose into a piece of cloth, she begged him to go on.

A little reluctantly Josiah continued. "Day after day I'd cry out to God to have mercy on me and heal me. I'd repent over and over of anything that I may have done to anger Him. I never felt God's condemnation though. In fact He was the only comfort I had." Rachel moved in maternally and, responding a little awkwardly, Josiah took a stick and poked the fire to revive it.

"I'd make a fire at night," Josiah continued, "and I'd sit close to avoid the chill of the night. He demonstrated, knees drawn up close, arms hugging them tightly. He began to rock. "Just like this and I'd sing the songs I'd learned as a child, while tears would stream down my face." Just for a moment Josiah looked uncomfortable (*have I shared too much vulnerability?* he thought), but looking again into Rachel's eyes, he knew it was safe.

"While you were away it seemed forever. But now you're back it doesn't seem so long," Rachel said.

"Days became weeks, weeks became months and the months blurred into years," Josiah responded. "Eventually it was only my sores that wept."

Rachel's eyes narrowed a little and her head moved back just a hint.

"Sorry," he continued, "but hopelessness hung around me every moment of every day. I was finding it increasingly hard to go on. Like the dying embers of one of my fires, life was slipping away and I could do nothing about it."

"And then, one day, intrigued by a commotion in the village,

I watched a crowd following someone I hadn't seen before. I couldn't hear what He was saying, but I watched Him intently as He talked to a man whom I recognized. To my amazement, I watched a man I'd known as a cripple all my life throw away his stick and walk freely and unaided."

"I heard about that," Rachel interjected. "Everyone was amazed."

"It *was* amazing," replied Josiah "I knew then for sure that God was with this Miracle-worker. As I watched the man's joy at his deliverance, I found myself filled with a burning hope, the like of which I'd never known before. If the Miracle-worker could do it for *that* man, then why not for me? Completely forgetting protocol, and with my eyes fixed on the Miracle-worker, I made my way towards the crowd."

Knowing the possible consequences of such an act, Rachel stared at Josiah in amazement. "I kept thinking to myself, 'What kind of Rabbi was this . . . who could do such incredible things?' "

Amazingly, I wasn't afraid. I just knew I had to get to the Miracle-worker and when I did, I immediately bowed down with my face to the ground.

"Please, Lord," I begged, now not daring to look at Him. "If You are willing You can make me clean." I could tell the crowd was visibly shaken by my impudence. Drawing back and covering their mouths and noses with their hands, they began to rebuke and curse me. Even the man who had been healed picked up his stick, began to point it aggressively at me and poked me to move me on, but I refused to budge.

"I just kept saying over and over, 'Lord, I know You can, please make me clean . . . if You are willing.' "

"All fell silent for a moment and I just felt I should sit up and I found the Miracle-worker looking right at me. Some in the crowd sniggered and laughed because dirt had stuck to my face and I must have looked hideous."

"The Miracle-worker touched me ... He *touched me* ... and, stunned, the crowd fell silent once again."

'I'm willing,' He said. 'Be healed!'

"Immediately I was clean. The vile affliction had gone. The Miracle-worker sent me to the priest and when he affirmed my healing, I came straight home."

Both Rachel and Josiah were beaming at the wonder of all that had happened.

The fire began to die down and they huddled together and stared at the star-filled sky. Josiah had seen those stars so often on his lonely nights, but had not previously had the eyes to see their beauty. Feeling a little overwhelmed he couldn't help but say, "My God, You are great!"

They sat in silence once again for a little while, until Rachel broke it by saying, "Time for bed, my husband?"

"Time for bed, my wife," Josiah agreed and he stood up and stretched.

"Just one more thing, Josiah," Rachel said. "Who was He and what was His name ... you know ... the Miracle-worker?"

Josiah, offering a hand to his wife, helped her to her feet and drew her close before kissing her gently on the lips. Slipping his arm around her waist, Josiah gently guided Rachel towards the house before answering. "They say He is the Son of God." He leaned in and kissed her head, "And His name? His name is ... Jesus."

✦ ✦ ✦

All men are most definitely *not* born equal, declares the caste system of the Indian Hindu. Everyone is born into a caste that is fixed for life and right at the bottom, the least of the least are the ones called the Untouchables. Considered impure, unclean and almost sub-human, they are not allowed to mix with the rest of society. It is forbidden to draw water from the same well or to eat or drink from the same utensils as anyone else. Excluded from temples they are shunned and abused wherever they go. A higher caste member would have to subject themselves to a thorough cleansing ritual if even the shadow of an untouchable should fall upon them. It is estimated that one out of six Indians, one hundred and sixty million people,[1] live their whole lives as outcasts.

I once visited a leper colony in Coimbatore, South India. Made outcasts by the misfortune of showing signs of infection, they had been forced from their homes and families and many were reduced to begging by the roadside. Some had lost their noses, or fingers or toes and in some cases all three. They had managed to recover some dignity at least though, as a local church, seeing their plight, had built them homes and made sure that they were fed. Without this they would have remained the victims of a society that ridiculed and rejected them.

Rejection by its nature has the roots of exclusion in it. This applies equally in different situations; to a group of friends in the school playground who decide you are no longer "in", or whole people groups are deemed not "in" because they are the wrong colour, or caste, or class, or whatever label you choose.

Since 2003, my family and I have been living in a nation that is recovering from the ravages of Apartheid. The "old" South Africa (as it is referred to now) was not unique in propagating a white-is-right society. What made it so abhorrent was that racial discrimination was legalized. Not too dissimilar from the Indian caste system, or the Third Reich, everyone was allocated status determined by the melanin level in your skin, the least pigmented "whites" at the top, the more you had, at the bottom.

Despite all the prophecies of doom, a new democracy emerged in 1994 and has thrived. Always quick to focus on the problems, the critics point the finger. But unless I've missed something, doesn't every nation have problems? Sure, the "First World" can sweep some of their issues under the carpet of wealth, but they're there all the same.

Recuperating from an evil and socially devastating system, South Africa is proving itself something of a phenomenon. Of course, white was never right and everyone else wrong. A society based on exclusion is doomed to failure. Jesus put it this way,

"Any kingdom divided against itself will be ruined."[2]

History shows us that rejection is random and reckless, whether you are Black, Jewish, Tutsi, Cambodian, Croat, female, old, physically challenged, a refugee, HIV positive . . . the list goes on and on.

What is it with this habit of putting someone else down so we can feel superior? Does it work? No. We fail to remember that we cannot diminish others without ourselves being diminished. Political correctness has done little more than drive our prejudice underground. Hiding behind correct terminology and a plastic smile, we bury our fear, but, sadly, the walls around our hearts remain intact.

Dr Christian Barnard, the famous South African cardiac surgeon, performed the first successful heart transplant on a human being. For this he will go down in history as making a significant contribution to medicine. Jesus, however, performs the kind of heart surgery that no human doctor can perform. Providing we sign the consent form, He will change our attitudes by renewing our minds. The power of His love unleashed upon even the most resistant heart can cause those walls to crumble.

We cannot change the past, but we *can* move on. We can build bridges where there have not previously been any and rebuild where pride and prejudice have washed them away.

Jesus had the power to simply say the Word and heal, yet in the account of Josiah's healing, we find that He *touched* him. Jesus showed us (as He did with the woman at the well) that His love transcends human imposed boundaries. He shows us that it *is* possible (quoting Diana Ross) to "Reach out and touch somebody's hand [and] make this world a better place".[3]

Mother Teresa said, "One of the greatest diseases is to be nobody to anybody."[4] Through Jesus we really do have the capacity to reach out to both the unloved *and* the unlovely. By being a conduit of Jesus' radical love, we face our fears and embrace all. We communicate a message of hope that *all*, without exception, have been made in the image of God and have immense value. Not least, because of that sweet sound of amazing grace, which cries out across the centuries from the cross of Calvary. A loving Saviour died once *and* for all.

Josiah had been physically afflicted by the disease he carried, but the deeper wounds of rejection were also healed by the touch of Jesus. There is healing in acceptance.

In a world where so many are ravaged by man's inhumanity to man, Jesus comes with a message of hope and healing to both the rejecter and the rejected. There's nothing mushy and sentimental about the huge challenges that this message presents. Forgiveness is central and essential to its success. Some toss this aside as idealism, maybe with good reason, as history provides us with a great breeding ground for cynicism.

But as for me, I have no choice but to tenaciously continue to hold on to the fact that *"God so loved the world that he gave his one and only Son."*[5] He came to a world that would utterly reject Him, but He came anyway in forgiveness and love.

Jesus throws a party for humanity, all are invited and all are welcome. The lonely, the disenfranchised, the lost, the broken, the disillusioned, the despised and rejected, everyone is invited. He loves the unlovable, accepts the unacceptable and touches the untouchable. Restoration and hope top the bill and the celebrations go on *forever*.

Let me tell you . . . *that* is one party you don't want to miss!

Notes

1. Figure sourced <http://magma.nationalgeographic.com>.
2. Luke 11:17
3. Lyrics by Nickolas Ashford and Valerie Simpson, © EMI Publishing
4. <www.brainyquote.com>.
5. John 3:16.

CHAPTER 8

PRESUMED DEAD
(Luke 7:11–16)

I had been in mourning for thirty days and for all of them I didn't know how I got out of bed in the morning. My husband's death was sudden. He had come home that evening and said that he felt unwell. If I had only known *that* was our last evening together, I would have done things so differently. As it was, I was grumpy and was going on about all the jobs that I had asked to be done around the house and they were still not done.

When I reflect now, he did look pale and he went to bed earlier than usual, partly I'm sure because he felt unwell and partly to escape my incessant nagging. He was a good man, kind, hard working and quieter than me. It's funny how the very things that had attracted me to him in the first place were the things that irritated me about him. I criticised him for being so predictable. Life was just work, home, synagogue, work, home and synagogue. Where was the excitement in our life? I don't know how I got to that place, but it just seemed so much easier to see all that was wrong, rather than all that was right.

He'd mumbled something about leaving early in the morning as he took himself off to bed and I didn't even bother to answer. In fact, I didn't even look at him, just to drive home the point that I wasn't happy. I do regret that! If only I had those moments again, I would do them so differently, but of course we didn't know.

He was sound asleep and breathing heavily as I climbed into bed and when I awoke he was still there. I shook him.

"I thought you were leaving early."

As soon as I touched him I knew something was wrong. He was so cold and stiff and then I realised he wasn't breathing. I panicked then and ran out onto the street screaming for help, and to be honest the rest is all a bit of a blur.

My saviour in it all has been my son. He had not long celebrated his bar mitzvah when his father died. We were so proud of him. For years we'd thought we couldn't have children. I miscarried twice and then God had mercy upon us and gave us a son. We used to joke that we were like Abraham and Sarah. In fact, that's why we called him Isaac, because he brought so much joy and laughter to us. He was never a strong child and would have attacks of shortness of breath. Many nights we would sit up with him applying poultices to his chest as he struggled to breathe. Sometimes I would see a certain look in his eyes that said, "Mum, can't you do something?" But neither I nor the doctors could do anything, well, except pray and we did much of that!

We hoped that he might grow out of it and indeed it did seem as though things became a little better but it was always there, waiting in the background to pounce at some inopportune moment. Despite his illness, he was our gift from God, our son, our Isaac.

With my husband gone, Isaac was all I had. He was so strong, he told me that he was going to look after me now and that everything was going to be alright!

I leaned on him, probably a little too much in the beginning. We were both hurting and it was actually too much for those young shoulders.

He was a lot like his father in his hard work and strength, but he was also a lot like me in his zest for life and fun. That made the sacrifice doubly hard – to stay at home and work when he would have loved to be out with his friends, doing the things young men do. But he never complained, well, not often anyway.

The work was hard and sometimes that weakness in his chest would recur and I would hear him coughing during the night. I wanted to help him – to at least rub some herbs or ointment in for him, but he wouldn't let me, because *now* he wanted to be the man.

For more than five years, we battled through and it seemed that finally we were turning a corner. I started to relax a little, even teasing him about a girl in the village who I knew liked him (her mother had told me so) and he would get all flustered and I'd laugh.

And then the crops failed! Apparently it was just one of those things, but that was little consolation. Something in my son broke that day. All that hard work, all that effort ... it would take years to recover from this blow. For the first time in a long time I saw *that* Mum-can't-you-do-something look in his eyes again.

It was vulnerability that I recognised. I'd seen it in the mirror many times. I don't know why there is such a fine line between celebration and devastation. Or why the light that separates you from complete darkness gets snuffed out in an unexpected and rogue gust of wind.

What I do know is something changed that day and hope just seemed to evaporate like a shallow pool in the heat of the sun. Isaac became sick, very sick. At first his breathing was bad only at night, but the lack of sleep meant that he was tired all day and soon he was sick more often than he was well. Going out to work in the fields became impossible for him and the little savings we had put by were used up. I was fearful. I was trying to be strong, but I was fearful. These days he let me rub his chest and sometimes at night, when it was really bad, I would sit next to him, because he couldn't lie down and he would rest his head on my shoulder and I would sing and pray while he hovered between wake and sleep.

And then there was *that* night. I awoke with a start as though from a nightmare, but far from leaving one, I was just about to enter one. It was as though the silence had woken me. I leapt from the bed and into Isaac's room and he was lying flat, his chest rising, falling and straining to fill his tired lungs with oxygen. The moonlight caught the beads of sweat on his forehead, which gave his already pale face a sort of deathly translucence. He half opened his eyes and weakly held out a limp hand for me to take hold of.

"Isaac ... Isaac ... what's wrong?"

He couldn't speak, he was too breathless. I took a cloth and gently dabbed the sweat from his forehead and he half-smiled his thanks. And then we made eye contact again. His eyes were sunken and framed by deep dark rings, but still managed to communicate their love.

"I love you, my son," I said as I held his hand and gently rubbed my thumb back and forth over it. There was a twitch in his lips that indicated he was trying to answer, but without averting his eyes from mine and with a final sigh, he was gone.

"God, no! No, God, please, have mercy God, not my son, not my Isaac!"

Erupting from deep within my soul came a desperate scream that brought the neighbours scurrying from their houses. I was inconsolable and the sound of weeping filled the night, making children cry in confusion and the dogs bark. My neighbours wept *with* me, but they also wept *for* me, for they knew that my future lay next to me, dead on the bed.

I just held onto his hand and cried out over and over,

"Why, God, why?"

I felt so utterly forsaken. Burying a husband was bad enough, but a mother was never meant to bury her child. My life was over. I would be reduced to begging on the streets. What had I done to deserve all this pain? I worked hard, I had given good offerings, I had always honoured God from being a child. I felt singled out and angry. Why was God being so cruel? If He wanted to kill me, why didn't He just kill me now, maybe then He could have taken me instead of my son. Why must I endure this tortured existence?

Out of the corner of my eye, I caught a glimpse of one neighbour in particular. I knew her to be a busybody and a gossip. She was also as mean as they come, but she had a son almost the same age as mine. She had her husband *and* her son (and a daughter for that matter). They weren't sick. They were strong and doing well. Why was God blessing them while I was in this living hell? Questions, spoken and unspoken, poured from every recess of my mind, but there were no answers coming back. It was as if they oozed from every pore of my body. I was awash in a sea of desperation with no sign of the shore.

Over the next few hours my neighbours and I wept as we prepared the body. As we did so, I became aware of how thin Isaac had become before he died; I hadn't really noticed it before. He'd grown to look so much like his father to add to my pain. I was haunted by flashbacks of recent events. Wave after relentless wave of emotion crashed over my soul as we placed him in the coffin and carried him through the village. We were quite a crowd as we headed towards the main gate. I don't know where I found the strength to walk. I felt like my stomach was caught in my throat and my legs were so very weak.

And then, unexpectedly, there was a change in the atmosphere. Crying had turned into something of a stifled excitement as we walked along. I looked up to notice a large crowd walking towards us. Who were they? What were they doing? I was

irritated by their insensitivity. Why couldn't they let me bury my
son with dignity? Must they interrupt so rudely?

At the front of the crowd I noticed one Man. It wasn't that He
was ahead of the others, yet at the same time I knew instinctively
He was the leader. He was staring at me. Well, I certainly must
have looked a sight. But it wasn't that. I was racking my brains to
think if I knew Him, but no, it wasn't that either. Now here is the
most ridiculous thing: in the midst of my pain, just in seeing Him
I felt hope bubble to the surface. My brain couldn't make sense of
it, but it was undeniable and irrepressible. I didn't say anything,
but He must have seen in my eyes distant echoes of my son's
silent plea,

"Sir, can't you do something?"

He came straight to me and I noticed He had tears in his
eyes. He spoke to me with words that were like a balm to my
soul,

"Don't cry!"

And in an instant I was able to stop. He walked right up to the
coffin and just touched it. The pall bearers stopped as did the two
crowds. What by all natural standards should have been an
awkward moment, wasn't; it seemed right somehow, like this
was supposed to happen. The man spoke to the body with great
authority and what was actually really bizarre felt absolutely
normal.

"Young man, I tell you to get up!"

My son – no word of a lie – sat up and began to speak. The
hushed sense of awe that had hung in the atmosphere prior to
this moment became pandemonium as everyone, including me,
drew back in shock and fear. Most were rooted to the spot, but a
few ran back to the village.

What magic was this? I thought, is this really my son? Our
eyes met and he looked healthier than he had in . . . well, ever.
And then he spoke directly to me,

"I love you too, Mum," and then he smiled the most glorious smile.

Too stunned to respond, I turned and looked at the Man.

"Who are You, sir?"

"I am Jesus," He replied. As the words left His lips, I fell to His feet and clung to Him. I just couldn't stop saying, "Thank You, thank You," over and over.

Jesus took my hand and lifted me up, then placed it in the hand of my son who was beaming from ear to ear. I immediately noted the strength of his grip, compared to the last time I had held his hand. I'm not sure what expression I was wearing, but my son laughed out loud and pulled me towards him and hugged me tight.

As I reflect on those life-changing moments (as I have done every day since they happened), I know now that what I thought was the end, was actually just the beginning! My nightmare was over; I was able to dream again. We met Jesus at the gate and passed from death to life.

Tragedy is no respecter of persons and always arrives untimely, uninvited and unwelcome. It doesn't always explode on the scene. Sometimes it surreptitiously creeps in and, like a coiled cobra, lashes out in places we didn't expect to find it. However it comes, its calling card is a branded soul. Even if, with time, some of the burning soreness eases, its mark is forever there.

Not everyone's story ends with an empty coffin. There are no easy answers to why it doesn't always work out that way. If there is a loving, all powerful God in heaven, who says He cares, why doesn't He prevent things like this happening? Maybe, like the woman we have read about, you have questions oozing from every pore for which you hear no response. And, though you may not like to admit it, you look around you and wonder why others (in your opinion far less deserving) are skating through life apparently problem free.

Could it be possible that sometimes we don't get the answers for which we long, because we ask the wrong questions? We write our internal journals of expectation, penning problem-free chapters, because *those* things happen to *other* people. Some of us like to think that we've got the ending of our stories all worked out, forgetting that we are not actually the author.

Whether we recognise Him or not, there is an Author of Life and He will never write anything into our story that He won't also give us enough strength to handle. The trouble with most of us is that when our story takes an unexpected turn, we draw conclusions that incorrectly pre-empt the end. Simply because you can't see it, it doesn't mean there isn't a happy ending.

A good friend, who I have known for a long time, sent me a book in the post recently. It was an old book, published in 1931 in fact, entitled *The Tragedy of Winston Churchill*.[1] It was a catalogue of the failures that had plagued Churchill's life, poking fun at and jeering at someone who had promised much and delivered little. Mr Churchill was already fifty-five years of age when it was published. Mr Victor Wallace Germains, the author, had made a common, but nevertheless serious, error. Churchill's finest hour, in fact all his finest years, were still ahead of him. History has re-written the story and cast Victor Germains' account into irrelevance. Years after the book was published, Churchill was Prime Minister of Great Britain and led the nation through the war with Nazi Germany. Rousing, faith-inspiring speeches flowed from formerly stammering lips. Against the odds, he championed the belief that victory was possible *and* it was. He caused a nation to believe that its finest hour was still ahead. The future contained not only Britain's finest hour . . . it also had Churchill's.

Like Winston Churchill, your ending may not be the one you, or others, anticipated. The characters and roles that are with you at the end of your story may not be the ones with whom you started out, but if you are still alive, then *your* story is still being written. Germains' book published Churchill's preparation, not his destination, and we must be careful not to do the same.

The thing about God is that He gives you an idea of the destination, but does not always let you know how He's going to get you there. You have to trust that He knows the way and you will arrive, but be warned, the way almost always involves passing through unexpected, even apparently dangerous terrain and usually takes longer than you would want. However, it must also be said that he doesn't force *His* ending on you. If you are determined to write your own destiny, He will let you, but are you really *that* confident that you know what's best for you? I doubt it!

Life, with all its ingredients, both bitter and sweet, is more than just the absence of death. When the death crowd met the life crowd, Jesus was not just someone who *can* resurrect the dead. He *is* the Resurrection; He's not just someone who *gives* life, He *is* Life.

Death and tragedy were no contest for His presence. Could it be possible that the burned out, charred remains of your dreams could be the now more fertile ground in which God will bring forth the harvest you once believed was possible? Some seeds only germinate once they have been scorched in the fire; the fire of your adversity is not the end and was never intended to be the end. You will yet emerge as the mythical phoenix or rather as the young Hebrew boys[2] from the flame and furnace, without even the smell of burning on you.

We're not talking about the end justifying the means, but we are saying whatever the hell and high water you've had to navigate, Jesus can and will see you through.

Many would consider scars to be ugly things, because they are uncomfortable reminders that all is not perfect in our world. I suggest that your scars mean that whatever tried to kill you didn't succeed. Those scars seen and unseen are striking and splendid trophies of your survival. Because Jesus *is* life, not a religious or philosophical alternative, He is the key to living. You will not die but **live** and declare the great things that God has done![3]

Surely there are few greater tragedies than to die having never really lived. If we want to really live, we need to give up trying to do life on our own. We are not here to merely exist until we expire. Jesus inspires us – breathes His life into us – to enable us to become more than the things we have become!

Give up trying to write your own story and, together with Jesus, make **his**-story!

Notes

1. Victor Wallace Germains, *The Tragedy of Winston Churchill*, 1931, Hurst and Blackett
2. Daniel 3:19–27 NLT.
3. Psalm 118:17 NLT.

CHAPTER 9

MAKING A STINK
(Luke 7:36–50)

The blanket loosely draped around her was clutched at the chest to stop it falling. She stuck her head out of the door and quickly looked up and down the narrow street. Pulling her head inside just as quickly, she said, "It's all clear."

He nodded and slipped into the night without looking back. When his footsteps faded she let the blanket fall to the floor and, surprised by the chill in the night air, she gave a shudder and quickly slipped into the linen garment in which she would sleep. Stepping over to the bed, she started to straighten it, pulling the sheets taught and plumping the pillows as if to erase all evidence of the evening's activity. She sat down at the dressing table, turned up the lamp, then picked up a comb and ran it through her hair, turning her head first on one side then tossing it all to the other. She replaced the comb. The money that had been left on the table apparently unnoticed, was carefully collected.

Swiftly and gracefully, she took a stool and stood on it to reach to the top of a cupboard. Hidden from view was a wooden box, which she carefully took down and then went through a practised ceremony. The box was placed on the table, next the oil lamp was drawn near in preparation. She went through this well-rehearsed ritual with an expression of focus and determination. Picking up a chair, she brought it over to the table and smoothed her night-dress under her as she sat down.

Carefully she pulled the box towards her into the light. She took a moment to stare at the lid of the box, ornate and beautifully carved, before taking hold of it. She removed the lid and tipped the contents out. A coin rolled out from the pile, bounced off the table, before rolling and finally spinning awkwardly on the packed earth floor. She watched it until it came to rest and then she got up and stooped to pick it up. Before returning to her seat, she pulled back the sackcloth curtain with a suddenness that suggested trying to catch a spy. Satisfied that no-one was hiding, she carefully arranged the curtains to cover the window once again.

Coin by coin she made little piles and meticulously placed them in a row. She counted them and for the first time her expression changed . . .

She almost smiled. Placing her arms horizontally on the table and her head on her hands, she was now eye to eye with her regimental display and satisfaction filled her eyes. She stayed in this position for some time, unmoving and allowing her eyes to rove up and down the rows. Suddenly, she took hold of the box and placed it under the lip of the table. Cupping her hand and with a sweeping motion, she scooped the coins back into the box. Standing on the chair once again, she replaced the box back out of view.

Collecting the oil lamp, she came to stand by her bed and yawned a huge yawn, only lifting the back of her hand to her mouth once it was all over. Still standing by the bed, she reached under the pillow and pulled out a long strip of cloth, which she used to tie her hair back from her face. At last, she climbed back between the sheets and reached across to snuff out the light. She waited only briefly for sleep to come, and the next thing she knew, it was morning.

The cock crowed and on the third crow, she opened her eyes.

Although the sackcloth curtain filtered the sunlight, it still forcefully filled the room. She squinted and covered her eyes with her hands. Intermittently she would check to see if the situation had improved, until eventually her eyes adjusted sufficiently to remove her hands completely.

Suddenly she sat up, and threw back the sheets with the sense of purpose of someone who remembered something important. She bathed, dressed and once again climbed onto the chair to retrieve her box. She wrapped it in a scarf and stepped out of her door into a quiet side street. Up a couple of steps and around the corner, she emerged into the main road, which was a very different story.

All hustle and bustle, market day brought traders from far and wide. As she wove her way through the crowd, passing a group of young men, she recognized a former client. She didn't make eye contact, but he had recognized her as there was an outburst of raucous laughter. This caused her usual reaction. Back straightened, she looked back over her shoulder. His friends were giving the young man back slaps of congratulation.

"Will you do the same for me?" one called out after her. She snapped her head back round and tried to melt into the crowd, but it was too late. Penetrating looks of disgust glared at her, but putting her head down, she kept going.

As she entered the market, she craned her neck as if to look for someone. At first, she didn't see what she was searching for. Then there he was ... the funny little trader with the gold earring and the turban. Bounding over to him, she had no sooner arrived than she blurted out,

"Do you still have it?"

The trader was deep in conversation and looked a little irritated at the sudden intrusion. However, his frown dissolved into a smile and a look of recognition as she repeated in a quieter voice, "Do you still have it?"

He did not say a word, but turned around and started to search for it. After a lengthy wait, the disappointment in her eyes caused him to stop teasing her and, for the first time, he spoke to her, "I don't think I've sold it." Reaching into a bag, he pulled out an exquisite marble vase. Pulling out the stopper, he bit his bottom lip to emphasize the care he was taking. Immediately, spicy perfume filled their nostrils. The trader sneezed.

"You do still have it." She smiled and went to take it, but the trader was too quick and she snatched at empty air. He rubbed his thumb and two forefingers together to indicate he wanted money.

She was angry now. She took the box out of its wrapper and held it towards him. He opened it and she watched him count out her earnings. Each of those coins had been bought dearly with self-esteem. They represented the men to whom she had given herself. Every tacky night she told herself this purchase would make her feel special. Now she held the vase and the extortionately expensive perfume that it contained. It had been a long time in the coming, but it was here at last and it was all hers. Only the richest of the rich could afford such an aroma. Owning something so expensive made her feel less cheap and inconsequential. Taking the silken scarf, she scrunched it up and put it inside her box. Next, she placed the perfume in the box, cradling it with the same care that a mother would place a sleeping baby in a cot.

After finding her way home again, she spent the day enamored with her purchase. She set it on the table next to her as she prepared herself for work. Painting her lips and eyes, she would catch herself delighting in her little perfume-filled marble vase.

The setting sun brought the end to the day and the tap on the door from her first client of the evening. She sighed deeply as she arose from the table and placed the vase next to the bed. As she worked, she could look at it and detach herself, briefly escaping to another world where she did not have to be what she was and do what she did.

It was not a busy night in spite of it having been market day and she was just about to prepare for sleep when another knock at the door told her she was not done after all. She decided to ignore it, but the knocking became all the more persistent. She opened the door and brazenly allowed her irritation to spill out of her mouth.

"No need to wake the whole street!" she barked.

Apologetic, a fresh-faced young man stood awkwardly shifting from foot to foot.

"Can I come in?" he said.

"Oh, very funny," she replied. "Your friends put you up to this, did they?" She shoved him to one side, looking for giggling youths and a fight, but there was no one there.

"Friends? I don't know what you mean," he said.

"Why are you here?" she asked sternly.

He didn't reply, but hung his head flushed with embarrassment.

"Just go home to mummy, son. There's nothing here for you."

She made to shut the door, but he reacted quickly and put out his hand to stop her. "Please, I have nowhere else to go!"

"Where do you live?" she asked.

"In Nain. I've travelled from Nain."

"Nain?

"I've come to find a man I know, but I haven't found him yet."

She found herself feeling sorry for him. He looked close to tears. It proved a mistake to look into those eyes once again, because she heard herself say, "Are you hungry?"

He smiled, nodding furiously. "Starving."

The smile fell away as she responded sarcastically, "Does this look like a restaurant?"

Crestfallen, he began to move away very slowly.

"I'm joking, ok? You sleep on the floor and be gone before dawn, take it or leave it."

Delighted, a smile broke out on his face, but she missed it, because she had already gone back inside. As he sheepishly followed her in, suddenly his senses were overloaded, his nose unaccustomed to the strong perfume and his eyes latched onto the pinks, purples and hints of gold of the flask. He was snapped back to reality though with the abrupt, "Sit!" as she pulled out a chair. He obeyed as she poured him a glass of wine and prepared him something to eat.

She wasn't really in the mood for making food or conversation, but she needn't have worried – as the wine diluted his shyness and loosened his tongue, he did most of the talking.

"You will never guess what happened in Nain last month. Nothing exciting ever happens in Nain, but I saw a miracle. I was watching the funeral of one of my neighbours. It was doubly sad because it was for the only son of a woman whose husband had died also. As the procession was on the way to the cemetery, a holy man called Jesus saw it and touched the body and the dead man came back to life! It's not every day you see someone raised from the dead . . . it was the talk of the town."

She found herself listening intently despite her efforts to ignore him. "He must have been just sleeping," she challenged.

"I probably would have thought the same," he replied, "but I was there. I watched life come back into a dead man. And that's why I'm here," he said.

"That's why you're *here?*"

"Yes, I heard that Jesus is here in town and I need to see Him again. I've heard He's doing miracles here now."

"Miracles, what kind of miracles?"

"The blind are seeing, the deaf are hearing and the cripples walk; people either reject Him as a fake or He changes their life altogether."

"Which camp are you in?" she asked as she placed stew and unleavened bread on the table before him.

"My life has completely changed since I met Him," he said.

Tearing off a hunk of bread, he began to dip it in the stew and eat with an eagerness that made her smile.

"How has your life changed?" she pressed.

There was a slight delay in his response as he chewed, swallowed and took a gulp of wine.

He continued to chew as he looked at her intently, assessing how she would receive what he was about to tell her.

"He makes you want to know God and to believe that God is able to help you. For instance, tonight I was wandering the streets, hungry and tired, nowhere to stay and I prayed ... yes, me ... I prayed."

Gripped by what he was saying, she probed, "What did you pray?"

"I prayed that God would find me a place to spend the night and, I can't explain it, but it was as though He showed me your door".

"Showed you my door ... what do you mean He showed you my door?"

"I don't know ... I just knew this was the right door on which to knock."

She was wide-eyed now. "So you didn't come for ... I mean because I'm a ... I mean do you know what I do?"

"What you do ... what do you mean, what you do? I came here because God showed me to come here. What do you do?" he said, half throwing stew laden bread in his mouth.

The naivety was sweet and unnerving all at the same time.

"Nothing, never mind," she said.

He continued talking, but she'd stopped listening ... could it really be possible that God knew where she lived? The thought both comforted and terrified her.

Just before dawn the next morning, he slipped away as promised after expressing his thanks with boyish gratitude. She, having tossed and turned her way through the night, hardly slept a wink, thinking about God and this holy man. She had to find Him. It wasn't rational but that was how she felt. She glanced at the vase by her bed, the pursuit of which had consumed her life. Yesterday, she could not take her eyes off it. Today, even *that* seemed shallow compared to finding *Jesus*.

She slipped it in her pocket and went out into the day. The morning sun, still low in the sky, was too bright for her tired eyes. She searched all morning and even asked God to help her find Him, but why should He listen to her? Tired and disappointed she almost turned for home, when two people passed her, whilst in deep discussion. They said that Jesus was at the house of the Pharisee known as Simon the leper.

Knowing the house and it not being too far away, she found it easily. Hovering outside, what was she to do? She fingered the vase in her pocket, seeing if it would somehow calm the heart that was pounding in her chest . . . it didn't.

No one was going to let her of all people in *that* house. This Pharisee knew who she was . . . he'd have her arrested or maybe worse.

"O God . . . I need a miracle," she prayed. No sooner had the words left her mouth than she stood as tall as she could and with a confidence that was not her own. She marched to the door, entered without knocking and stood in the doorway.

The confidence with which she'd entered immediately evaporated and she froze, mesmerized by the all the eyes that turned to look at her. Too shocked to do anything, no-one moved.

Over at the table she instinctively knew that the one reclining with His back to her was the holy man they called Jesus. In fact, *He* was the only one not staring at her. Courage from she knew not where seeped back into her heart, allowing her body to move towards Him. Though she had every reason to be afraid, she wasn't.

In the sweetness of His presence, she became overwhelmed by the bitterness of her life. In a moment when, for the first time, everything seemed so right, she was shaken by her own wrongness. Exposed, vulnerable in the truth, but she resisted the temptation to run. A dam of pent-up emotion and sorrow broke within and heavy tears, like the first drops of rain in a storm . . . pit . . . pat . . . fell on Jesus' feet. Hastily she released her loosely plaited hair and gave it a shake as she fell to her knees. Taking it in her hands, she wiped His feet with her hair, drying the tears that were instantly replaced with more.

She'd been alone with many men and found that she'd never experienced intimacy like she was feeling now, even with a room full of scowling people. There was just something about being close to Him.

It was the gasp, as she began to kiss His feet, which reminded her again that she had an audience. Some turned away in horror; one or two looked poised to do something and yet did not move. And Him? He lay unmoved; she couldn't see His eyes, but she could feel them watching her every move. She'd never met Him before, but she knew that He not only knew where she lived, but everything about her. He could have turned away and yet chose not to. She couldn't help but express her sorrow and as she kissed His feet, she whispered, "I'm sorry," over and over again.

She had been so aware of her guilt, but now she became aware that a huge weight had left her shoulders. She felt clean and free; gratitude welled up within her. How could she express her love? How could she ever say "thank you"? Reaching into her pocket, she took out the jar. Her hands were shaking and perspiring and she wiped one on her clothing, so that she would have sufficient grip to release the stopper. It came out all of a sudden, which meant that some of the fragrant contents splashed on Jesus' feet.

Now for the first time she looked into His eyes, expecting a rebuke for her clumsiness, but there was no hint of admonishment. Still looking into His eyes, she now began to pour the perfume over His feet. Without considering its cost, she poured her thank-offering out before Him, its preciousness paling into insignificance compared to what He had given her.

Right there in that room, caught in the glare of despising eyes, salvation, unannounced and unexpected as she had been, was visiting. Unseen, yet very real fetters were broken and she was free. As the aroma of the sweet, spicy fragrance permeated the atmosphere, so did the muttering, gasps and objections.

Speaking for the first time and without looking away, He defended her before them and told her what her heart already knew, her many sins were forgiven.

Catching the eye of the host, she noticed his gaze drop immediately. He hated everything she was. Everything he knew told him her uncleanness made her unwelcome ... an outcast. Now the roles were reversed, she pitied him because Salvation had come to his house, right before his very eyes and he'd missed Him.

As she stood, her vase fell from her lap to the floor, rolling into the corner. She watched it go and then turned to look at Jesus. Her little vase had meant so much and now it meant nothing. She had become the vessel that contained something so much more precious. She rejoiced that God knew where she lived and had come to seek her out.

"Your faith has saved you," He said. "Go in peace" ... and she did.

✤ ✤ ✤

If we could make ourselves right, wouldn't we have done it by now? So often we know what needs to be done and yet we lack the ability to turn knowledge into action. Diets start Monday and fade by Friday, because our moment by moment decisions so powerfully affect the momentum towards success or failure.

My wife and I made a foolish pact in our early twenties. I say foolish, because I was making decisions in the dark that would look so different in the light. Our pact was that we would stay fit and thin for each other. Now you may well be able to wax lyrical about the virtues of cuddly, but this was our naïve promise.

Two decades have come and gone and the pounds have come and *not* gone, which led my wife, God bless her, to buying me some sessions with a personal trainer for my forty-fourth birthday. So sweet! Please allow me a moment to share three things I've learned through the hours of sweat and pain.

First, behind the charm and smile of my personal trainer lies the heart of a sadist. That has no relevance to what I have to say ... I just wanted you to know.

Second, I'm clearly not the greatest judge of my ability ... or more pointedly ... my capacity. I have gone to the gym for years and thought myself to be reasonably fit, but was often frustrated by my lack of progress. I have learned that boundaries that are not pushed stay where they are or may even recede. What was formerly my work-out has become my warm-up. I have learned that though I went kicking, screaming and grunting all the way ... I am capable of far more than I thought I was.

Thirdly, pain is part of progress. Comfort zones are not the arena for great and lasting change in our lives. If we want the prize, then we must be prepared to pay the price.

Joining a gym doesn't make me fit; I actually have to go *and* use the equipment effectively. Personal trainers are great, but if all has gone to plan, *they* are not the ones swimming in sweat at the end of the session. I had to do something to access his knowledge and expertise. I had to be present, I had to listen and I had to do what he said. I had to trust that he knew what I was capable of and what was best for me – more than I did. And though I was exhausted and it was hurting like hell and my body was screaming *"Stop!"* I just had to keep going. Why? Because though progress is sometimes slow, I can tell you that I'm purchasing a stronger fitter, healthier more energetic body with all that pain.

We'll never really know the events that led to a prostitute scandalously having the bottle to walk into a Pharisee's house uninvited. We do know, however, that she had grasped who Jesus was and what He was capable of. Was she the only person in the room that day that required forgiveness? Absolutely not! But we know this ... she desperately wanted to change, she was prepared to face derision and even risk punishment in order to get to Jesus. She manifested an extravagance which expressed the depth of her desire and drew huge criticism. The fact is, it only seemed extravagant to those who did not understand the value of the One who was sat amongst them.

It *was* perfectly appropriate for her to bring what was probably the most valuable thing she owned and splash out on Jesus. Far from agreeing with the crowd, as usual Jesus saw beyond the obvious, and explained that it is normal for those who have been forgiven much to express their love and gratitude *extravagantly*.

Refusing to accept the status quo, refusing to just accept her lot in life, she believed change was possible and put legs to that belief. No wonder Jesus said to her, *"Your* faith has saved you" (emphasis added). In essence, He was telling her that she was receiving the prize of her audacious faith.

Even beyond Jesus, I believe that *this* act of worship and contrition affected all, irrespective of their opinions. The fragrance released that day was so strong that it overpowered the stench of their attitude. It permeated the house, and got into their hair and the fabric of their clothes. They all carried a reminder of that encounter away with them.

Change *is* possible, but at a price. I have to do something to access Jesus. I have to listen and to do what He says. I learn what to do through prayer and reading His Word, the Bible. I have to trust that He knows better than I what I am capable of and what is best for me. I choose to trust even when I'm exhausted and it hurts like hell and everything within me is screaming *"Stop!"* I will keep going. Why? Because He takes me from *my* strength to *His* strength. He is extending my boundaries and increasing my capacity.

God isn't looking for perfection, but there *is* something about passion and extravagance that catches and holds His attention. Seizing the opportunity to disapprove and criticise, other people will often seek to stifle and smother your zeal. Enthusiasm makes people uneasy and it's easier for them to try to hinder you than deal with their own apathy.

Deciding to change your life and *not* follow the crowd may not make you popular. It almost certainly won't be easy and may cost you all that you consider most precious. But the prize *is* worth the price. Be bold and true to yourself. Submit to God and all He has laid upon your heart. You will release a glorious fragrance that makes a lasting impression on everybody.

What kind of stink are you making?

CHAPTER 10

NAILED
(Luke 23:26–43)

"Death!" was my sentence and the last word that came out of the Judge's mouth. Dragged unceremoniously from the courtroom, I was tossed like a piece of garbage onto the straw covered floor of one of the cells. Lifting my head after a moment, I spat straw from my mouth and looked around at the eyes which were staring back at me. Dead and expressionless faces soon lost what could be loosely described as interest in my arrival. I shuffled so that my back was against a wall. From here I surveyed the condemned who, like me, awaited their fate.

Condemned ... I pondered the fact that I was going to die. There had been many times in my sad existence that I'd wished I were dead and now that it was going to happen, ironically, I wanted to live.

The heat and the stench of the prison were overwhelming, but both were overpowered by the fear that dried my mouth and knotted my stomach. I wanted to cry, but no tears came. The lump in my throat peaked with pain, subsided slightly and then just sat there and would not be swallowed away.

Noticing some water over near the wooden door, I made my way to it. There was barely anything in the pot and what *was* there had straw floating on top and gritty sediment at the bottom. It tasted foul, but at least the moisture brought a modicum of relief to my parched throat.

As once again I took my place, I watched the sun stream in through the high, narrow window. Dust danced and swirled in its beam. And the flies . . . my God, the flies . . . darted in and out of the rays.

Surprised by anger, I allowed the thoughts it generated to further fuel its flame. Why had it come to this? Why had I been so stupid? Why was life so very unfair? Why did I get caught? I was just going to do one more job and this time I'd meant it. The owners of the house had turned up unexpectedly early and I was caught red-handed! Involuntarily, a cry of frustration escaped my lips and caused a moment of uneasiness in the cell.

I felt so desperate. I remembered my Grandmother, whose hands alone could bring the comfort I needed right now. I lifted my hand to my face, pointlessly seeking to simulate the experience, but to no avail.

My parents both died when I was young and I had only hazy recollections of them. Grandmother's husband had died before I was born and she had brought me up on her own. She was a kind woman, but was no longer young and was not strong enough to handle me when muscle and the desire to have my own way grew. I can't really remember how my getting into trouble started, but it did. All my friends had stuff we couldn't afford, most of it liberated from someone else, and Gran was just *too* old to keep up, I suppose. She never asked questions as to where I had got the things that I'd brought home and I never told her.

She would sit sewing and humming in the evenings, and when I was younger I'd kneel at her feet and rest my head on her lap. She'd always stop sewing and keep humming whilst gently stroking my hair. In those moments I felt such comfort and peace that I'd often drift off to sleep, whereupon she'd gently wake me and send me to my bed.

I'd have sent her to her grave if she'd been alive today. So I was left with the dilemma of wishing she was alive and being glad she wasn't. I was snapped out of my daydreaming by an insistent sensation. I began to scratch my legs furiously as fleas dined upon them. I seemed to itch everywhere. In utter frustration I tapped and then rhythmically knocked my head on the wall against which I leaned. The pain brought a welcome, but only temporary distraction to my torment.

The only other break in the monotony was when a guard tipped a pail of water into our water pot and threw lumps of stale bread on the floor. Like a pack of starving dogs, all the able-bodied would fight to take their share of the meagre offering. This was always the most activity I'd see from the other inmates, but it was only a short-lived flurry. I'd been too slow to get anything, but I wasn't hungry. When I returned to the water pot after the feeding frenzy, it had been reduced to the usual vile crumb, straw and grit concoction.

The temperature plummeted as day dissolved into night. I shivered with knees drawn up around my chest and watched as the cell intermittently became flooded with moonlight and then plunged into darkness as passing clouds snuffed out its brightness. I don't know when I fell asleep, but mercifully I did and was awoken by a bird singing somewhere near our only window. I could have imagined myself being immensely irritated by such a sound on any other day, but today its sweetness invaded my soul. And then it was gone, snatched away in a moment like a warm blanket on a winter's day.

I knew that this was the day that I was supposed to die, but death is hard to imagine when you're still alive. What would God do with me? I was a miserable sinner . . . a reprobate . . . how could I ever hope to make peace with Him? I thought about praying, but the words just wouldn't come.

The heavy wooden door swung open with considerable force.

Two guards, after the briefest of glances around the cell, grabbed me. I tried to struggle, but they were used to it and just dragged me out of the door. My resistance ceased as I was overwhelmed by the sight before me. They'd just finished with another guy who looked like a piece of meat. They had just cut Him free from a post in the centre of the courtyard. His whole body was covered in blood and He had a ring of thorns shoved on His head. Terror gripped my heart and raced and pounded in my chest. My whole body shook with anticipation and then it was my turn for blow after body-wrenching blow.

Cold water hit my face and brought me round. The coughing and sputtering brought pain like a million knives being plunged into my back. I was dragged away, legs trailing in the dirt, to the sound of screams and cursing coming from the next occupier of the post.

Drifting in and out of consciousness, I heard the soldiers screaming at me, "Take hold of it! Take hold of it!" The weight of the heavy tree trunk they laid on me chafed my weeping, tender back. The man ahead of me was the one with the thorns and people were screaming at Him, waving fists in His face and spitting on Him. I don't know what He'd done but it must have been bad, I thought. Yet I was also confused, because, in spite of the angry mob, several women were weeping, unashamedly showing their love and anguish at His suffering.

The exertion and pain caused me to stop and retch – but there was nothing in my stomach. Up ahead, the man with the thorns kept collapsing, His strength was giving out. He didn't look like He could walk one step, never mind any further. One of the soldiers pulled a man out of the crowd to carry His spar. I was angry and started to shout, "Hey, what about m . . . ?" The anger caught in my throat and made me cough. The crosspiece I was carrying bounced on my back and pain caused my legs to give way. The soldiers kept yelling at me "You! Keep going!" Forcing myself to stand, I lost sight of the Man with the thorns as the crowd closed in behind Him. I staggered and stumbled my way to the place they called The Skull.

I let go of the heavy wood. It bounced in the dirt and the soldiers fixed it to another, longer piece. While they were doing that, I saw the charge: "King of the Jews", nailed on Thorn Man's cross. I was forced down upon my tree. Each time the hammer went clink . . . clink . . . I could hear myself and the scrunch of nail jarred through bone.

The atmosphere was thick with mocking and hatred. Drunk with pain, I came in and out of consciousness as the cross was raised. The foreign occupiers knew what they were doing. I couldn't breathe out unless I forced my knees to straighten against the nail in my heels. Before, I'd feared death . . . but now I wanted it to come quickly and release me from my torment.

Women wept and wailed under the cross of the Man with the thorns on His head – but no-one wept for me. Loneliness and terror taunted me like a rabid dog.

Then I heard Him speak, loudly (how did He have the strength now?) "Father, forgive them . . . they don't know what they are doing." Could it be true that He was forgiving those who were taking His life? I turned to look at Him, He was looking back at me and even through the swelling and the blood it was as though those eyes pierced my soul. His innocence was immediately obvious to me, as was my guilt. I couldn't know for sure that He *was* who they said He was, but it seemed He had power after His prayer. Soldiers gambled on the ground for His clothing and others called out, "You've saved others. If You are the Son of God save Yourself!" Somehow, I was filled with hope that the man with the thorns on His head could indeed be God's Son.

The other guy who was crucified with us joined in the insults, "Come on, save us and Yourself."

I found indignation rise up in me. With a strength that came from I know not where, I cried out, "Shut up, you fool! Do you not fear God? We're guilty and getting what we deserve, but this man is innocent." I had to stop, as agony forced air back into my lungs, but now I found myself utterly convinced that Jesus *was* indeed the Son of God. I had to try and talk just once more.

"Please, Jesus."

As I spoke, Jesus once again looked at me.

"Remember me when You come into Your kingdom." There was a love that exuded from Him that I had never felt before. It reminded me of my Grandmother humming and stroking my hair – only stronger, more wonderful. He looked at me again and though His mouth didn't move, I saw a smile in His eyes. With a voice that was barely audible He said, "Today, you will be with Me in Paradise."

Hit by a wave of forgiveness, tears stung my eyes and dripped from my chin. I felt clean and almost anaesthetised by peace. I knew it was well with my soul. I had no idea where Paradise was, but if He was going to be there . . . that's exactly where I wanted to be.

Guilt is a terrible thing. We can understand that people can sometimes do such terrible things they deserve punishment. But there are no great or bad people born anywhere, just babies. The journey to perpetrator is preceded by a history, often of extreme childhood mistreatment. That said, unless someone is suffering from mental illness, people need to be held accountable for their own sin.

I remember that as children, when my sister and I were having a fight, I was physically stronger, but she was more of a strategist. One day she picked up a bottle of cheap perfume that was a gift from Grandmother, sprayed me and ran off. Not to be outdone, I took the nozzle off the atomiser, caught up with her, and with one sharp flick of the wrist a stream of nauseating liquid flew through the air. It landed ... not on the intended target, but on a recently decorated wall and my mother's prized painting of a bowl of fruit. You might think, like I did, this was no big deal and what was needed was to rethink my retaliation. But priorities changed when, to my horror, Grandma's perfume began to eat its way through the paint on the wall and the painting. *That* was the moment I realised I was dead meat and if my father found out it would be curtains.

Armed with crayons, felt tips and a good measure of desperation, I managed to make an already bad situation much worse. Panic began to settle in, but I talked to myself firmly and told myself that it wasn't *that* bad and that Dad would understand. I'd done a pretty good job of calming myself down when my brother walked by ... gasped and said, "Oh my word, Dad is going to kill you!" From that moment my life became consumed with fear of discovery.

A week or two went by with nothing being said, which lulled me into a false sense of security. That is until one night. Lying in my bed waiting for sleep, I heard my father walk down the hall past the mess. As I remember, there was coughing, spluttering and other sounds of outrage as he was fully impacted by his discovery. He came up the stairs, into my bedroom where I lay motionless, "asleep".

My Oscar winning performance only postponed things until morning. Though the thought of denying everything *had* occurred to me, in the end I decided to come clean. (The astute among you will have worked out by now that the rumours of my imminent demise had been grossly exaggerated.) However, my popularity ratings went south and didn't improve for some considerable time.

There *was* a degree of relief that I was no longer *waiting* to be found out. Guilt, however, still clung to me like a leech. It had been an unintended mistake, but I had been caught up in the moment and had not stopped to consider the consequences. Sure, I had been incited, but no one was concerned about that. It was *my* actions that had irreversible effects over which I had no control.

Grace is amazing. It comes looking for us when we are guilty and lifts us up when we least deserve it. Covering our shame, it is there to comfort us when the dawn of realisation comes ... again. Human beings are not designed to carry guilt; when we do, it is always damaging. Grace is not there to excuse us when restitution is required, it leads us to acknowledgement of our wrongdoing and it delivers us from a weight that is too much for us to carry alone.

When I was about ten years of age, I was visiting my other Grandmother with my brother and sister. It was lunch time and Grandma placed a large jug of milk on the table. I don't know what came over me, but in *another* moment of insanity I poured sugar into the milk. I think my sister blew the whistle and my sweet, sweet Grandma turned into the Incredible Hulk. She told my mother and if Grandma was angry, Mum was furious. This time I was going to pay. I don't know why, possibly he had discovered he could reduce nuclear anger explosions going on around him, youngest children often learn appeasement strategies, but my younger brother said, "I did it."

I could hardly believe my ears. He hadn't realised the consequences of his selfless act, but Mum bent him over a stool and prepared to give him a hiding. I would love to tell you that nobility won the day and before the deed could be done I stepped up to the plate and owned up, but I didn't. I'd done the crime, but I stood and watched as my brother took the punishment that should have been mine.

The incredible message of the Cross is that Jesus, the man with the thorns who is utterly innocent, takes the punishment we should be having, and not just for the sugar-in-the-milk stuff; every conceivable (and even inconceivable) vileness, He paid for. Fully knowing the consequences, He takes the guilt from our shoulders and places it squarely on His own. For everything we *have* done and everything we *will* do ... now that's grace!

Grace is both a powerful and a dangerous message. The danger is that some could abuse it, using grace as an excuse to keep doing something they should have stopped.

Some years ago I remember hearing the story of some prisoners of war who had been kept in a darkened bunker for years. Upon liberation, the prisoners stepped out, blinking into the daylight. After a few minutes, to the astonishment of their rescuers, they went back inside the bunker.

It was never the intention of the Grace Giver to keep rescuing us from the darkness, but rather to keep us walking in the light.

Are you hoarding secrets – or hiding skeletons in the cupboard? Have you messed up and found yourself bearing the weight of a host of unintended consequences? Maybe *you've* had experiences that have changed the course of your life and left you treading water in a sea of regret. If you have then that makes you a member of a not so exclusive club called the human race. We've all failed in one way or another. We've all missed it and messed up. Jesus doesn't turn up in our lives Mary Poppins' style bringing instant order to chaos with a wiggle of the nose and a wag of the finger. This is definitely a magic wand-free zone. It can take time to turn things around and it usually does. In the process we have to remember that failure is an event, not a person. Recovery is possible. We can choose *not* to be defined by our mess.

A religious fanatic, Saul of Tarsus, dragged professing Christians off to prison. He had watched, giving his full assent, as they murdered Stephen, a follower of Jesus. A first-hand encounter with Christ on the road to Damascus literally knocked Saul off his feet. He got up a transformed man to become Paul the Apostle who wrote the majority of the New Testament. Thank God, Paul did not live life looking in his rear view mirror. He pressed on, so that he might grasp hold of all that God had got for him. God helps us deal with all the stinking thinking that got us into the mess in the first place and then helps us live free. Jesus gave His all, so that you could give your all.

Our mutual enemy, who is seeking to insert as much pain, disappointment and shame into our lives as possible, is fighting us today for what God wants to give us tomorrow. If he (the enemy) can just get me to focus on me then he can paralyse me with shame and regret. But if I focus on Him (Jesus) and all that He's done, then it is possible to step out of the darkness and into the light, unleashing previously untapped potential. It probably sounds too good to be true. Well, as millions would testify, it is good and it is true! Love and divine acceptance awaits us, not just in spite of our baggage, but with it.

Will you respond to the man with the thorns on His head? Does the thought of clearing out your junk and starting again appeal to you?

Being nailed by grace means you will discover the person you were born to be and the life you were meant to live. *So what are you waiting for?*

About the Author

Originally from the UK, Malcolm Baxter served in full-time ministry for over fifteen years in a thriving, thousand member strong city church. He has travelled extensively, speaking at churches and conferences in many different nations. After planting a church in his home town, he and his family received the call of God to go to South Africa where he now leads a church in Cape Town with his wife, Lynette. Malcolm and Lynette have four children, Bethany, Aaron, Joseph and Gabrielle.

We hope you enjoyed reading this New Wine book.
For details of other New Wine books
and a range of 2,000 titles from other
Word and Spirit publishers visit our website:
www.newwineministries.co.uk
email: newwine@xalt.co.uk